Evangelism for a New Age

John Drane is Director of the Centre for
the Study of Christianity and Contemporary Society at the University of Stirling,
and is the author of numerous books,
including *What is the New Age Saying to
the Church?*

Available from Marshall Pickering
By the same author

What is the New Age Saying to the Church?

Evangelism for a New Age

Creating Churches for the next Century

JOHN DRANE

Marshall Pickering
An Imprint of HarperCollinsPublishers

Marshall Pickering is an Imprint of
HarperCollins*Religious*
Part of HarperCollins*Publishers*
77–85 Fulham Palace Road
Hammersmith, London W6 8JB

First published in Great Britain
in 1994 by Marshall Pickering

1 3 5 7 9 10 8 6 4 2

A catalogue record for this book
is available from the British Library

ISBN 0 551 02843-2

Printed and bound in Great Britain by
HarperCollinsManufacturing Glasgow

Contents

Preface

The origins of this book go back at least ten years, to 1984 when I was invited to become Mission Convener of the Scottish Churches Council. Few people find spiritual renewal by joining church committees, but as I look back over those ten years I have no doubt that is what happened to me. In 1984 I was a traditional academic, trained to do theology the way others had done it for centuries before me. I was reasonably good at it, and had written a number of books on the Bible to prove it. But as I got down to the business of working out what we would need to be and do to share the Christian faith effectively at the end of the twentieth century, I soon discovered that I had a lot to learn – about myself, about contemporary culture, about the world Church, and about God. It is a truism to say that we are all in the process of becoming someone, but there can be no question that as I have worked through these and other related issues, I have become a very different person from what I was before. I still have a lot to learn, but just now, almost midway through the 'Decade of Evangelism', seems the right time to share with the wider Church some of what I think I have discovered.

The opportunity to put my ideas into some kind of coherent form first came in 1989 when my friend Raymond Fung, who was then Evangelism Secretary to the World Council of

Churches, invited my wife Olive and me to join him for a
series of international Schools of Evangelism that he was planning. The first of them took place in Adelaide, Australia in
July 1990. At the time what I had to say seemed to me so commonplace and obvious that I wondered how it could be worth
travelling halfway round the world to say it. But I forgot that
by then I had been living with these thoughts for a few years,
and what was commonplace to me was new to others. What I
had to share was given such a warm reception that I soon realized it had the potential to become a significant alternative
model for evangelism as we approach the new millennium. I
was particularly encouraged by the response not just from
western church leaders (some of whose churches are in such
serious decline that they would grasp at anything), but also
from the leaders of huge and fast-growing churches in places
like Korea, Africa, Malaysia and South America. Since 1990,
I have had the opportunity to present this material in a wide
variety of different contexts, evangelical as well as ecumenical, academic as well as ecclesiastical, and always with the
same positive response. If it is genuinely a new model for
evangelism, then I can only say it is also a return to our historical origins, for it is rooted in the teaching and practice of
Jesus. It is also a reflection of the experience of the world
Church, and for many of its insights I am indebted to non-
western Christians, not least Raymond Fung himself.

   This is not a 'how-to' book that will provide blueprints of
evangelizing strategies, though I have no shortage of specific
ideas as to how its principles can be put into practice. Much
of my time in recent years has been taken up working with my
wife and partner, Olive, leading workshops in churches and
seminaries all over the world, exploring what this model would

look like in different contexts. But what works for one church is not necessarily going to work somewhere else. Congregations can waste much time and energy trying to copy others. This is why the focus here is on an overall approach to and understanding of evangelism, that can easily be transferred from one culture to another, whereas specific ideas generally cannot. Moreover, I believe that a particular set of attitudes can be identified from within the New Testament itself, especially in the teaching and example of Jesus, and that these attitudes are in any case sufficiently distinctive to justify a book to themselves.

Few academic theologians ever get around to writing a book on evangelism. We seem to have persuaded ourselves that theology and evangelism are two entirely different enterprises, the one being objective and detached, the other being subjective and confessional. The study of evangelism does not sit easily within the context of western theological education, though there are exceptions. Fuller Seminary in Pasadena, California, USA, invited Olive and me to teach a regular course for them, EV 509: Spirituality and Creativity for Evangelism and Worship, and the need to provide resources for that gave some impetus to the writing of this book, as well as personal encouragement to us both. But the British academic world still generally accepts the view that anyone with specific religious commitments is unlikely to be able to exercise any critical judgement about any topic related to those commitments. It never seems to work that way for atheists, of course, but when Christians write about Christianity it is generally assumed that their 'bias' will inevitably determine their conclusions. Since evangelism is by definition concerned with how to communicate and commend Christian faith to those who are not yet believers, the authors of books like this one must suffer from a double disability. I explain all this so that readers will understand where I am coming from. I can only be who I am, though I recognize that some people will find my insistence on critical scholarship irksome, while others will find my use of popular materials uncritical.

Finally, it will be worth saying that you are missing the point if you read this book as a negative assessment of western Christianity. Of course there are awkward questions we need to face. But there are plenty of things in our heritage of which we can be proud. There is nothing wrong with many of the things we now do. But a lot of churches are like a glass that is only half full. Most of what is in the glass is good, wholesome and profitable – at least for those who are already church members. The problem is not so much with the half that is full, but the half that is empty. If I have not referred much to what we already have – whether in terms of belief or practice – that is not because I don't believe it, or don't like it, but because I assume we can take it for granted. This book is about some things that, for whatever reason, we have missed or forgotten – but which are fundamental to the evangelizing dynamic as we find it in the New Testament, and as we will need to rediscover it if we are to create churches that will be effective in the 21st century.

John Drane
Advent 1993

chapter one | Faith, Culture and the 21st Century

In case you have failed to notice it, the dawn of the 21st century is just around the corner. From time immemorial, the start of a new century has always been a thought-provoking occasion. It is a time for reflection on what is past, for a sense of pride in some of the good things that have happened in our generation and those of our parents and grandparents. It is also the occasion for regret, as people reflect on the hopes and aspirations that went unfulfilled, and on the mistakes that were made. All those feelings are in evidence as we approach the end of the 20th century. There is alarm at the way human life and well-being has so often been threatened by the very inventions that were supposed to improve it all, and yet (to paraphrase a well-known Christmas carol), the hopes and fear of many years are coming together in a new spirit of expectancy as people throughout the world prepare to close an old chapter and begin a new one.

Wherever we look, people's horizons are being widened, and their vision inspired by the realization that a new age is about to dawn, and maybe this time we will get it right. Indeed, the possibilities this time around seem so much greater than they have ever been. Of all the generations that have gone before us, we are uniquely privileged not just to stand on the threshold of a new century, but of a new millennium. In all the centuries there have been since people started counting time in the way we do now, only one generation before us has initiated a new millennium, and that was a long, long time ago, when the year 999 gave way to the year 1000. Well, maybe not, for there has been some debate as to exactly when a new millennium truly begins. The consensus of informed opinion is that the 20th century will not officially end until 31 December 2000, which means the next millennium starts at midnight on 31 December 2000. Notwithstanding all that, no one need doubt when the partying will start: New Year's Eve 1999, and hotels and public buildings around the world are already booked up in anticipation! Multitudes of people are looking forward to the big day, and as it comes ever closer we can only expect an intensification, not just of the celebration but also of the serious questions that human beings will have to face in the 21st century. As we begin to limber up for the starter's pistol, more and more people are trying to gaze into the future to discern the trends that will shape the way we run our lives in the new century. Big business is already planning millennial marketing strategies, and the hype is about to begin. Of course, it's not all exciting news. The scenario described so far is very western – and prosperous western at that. For other people, their deepest aspiration is that the dawn of a new century might bring an end to the suffering and injustice imposed on them by corrupt warlords and politicians, and their cry for fairness finds a ready echo among many thinking westerners, who are questioning the very fabric of civilization as we have known it for the past three or four centuries. At the same time, those for whom the next century means the most – today's children –

can often be heard wondering if there will be a future for them, or whether it is yet another cruel illusion, and instead of ushering in a golden age, the 21st century might see the whole world system fall helplessly into the abyss of ultimate environmental disaster.

People have always had an insatiable appetite for knowledge of the future. Every significant civilization of the ancient world had its soothsayers and astrologers. Kings were unable to rule without their constant support, armies never went into battle without first consulting them, and ordinary people were both inspired and terrified by their apparently supernatural power to look beyond the mundane and the everyday and to see the bigger picture that had its effect on everyone's lives. A thousand years ago, as the first Christian millennium was about to give way to the second, there was much feverish speculation about when the world would end, while the last 150 years have seen any number of groups all asking the same question. Most have flourished for a time, and then disappeared. Some – such as the Plymouth Brethren – sprang up within the framework of the Christian Church, and have since lost their apocalyptic distinctiveness by merging with the Establishment to become just another church. Others, such as the Theosophical Society established in the mid-19th century by Helena Blavatsky, sprang from different spiritual roots, but they too have been domesticated and accepted as part of the religious (albeit non-Christian) scene. A few have fallen into the control of dangerous autocrats like David Koresh, the self-styled 'messiah' of the Branch Davidian sect that was annihilated in a spectacular fireball at their Waco, Texas headquarters in early 1993.

NEW QUESTIONS –
AND SURPRISING ANSWERS

Historically, people who were attracted to join such groups
have been ordinary people who were just apprehensive about
what the future might hold. Many of them have been loners
who for a variety of reasons found themselves on the fringes of
western culture. But that is no longer the case. As we
approach the end of the 20th century, such activity has inten-
sified rather than diminished. The London *Financial Times*
regularly carries adverts from clairvoyants who offer advice
about how money can be invested in stocks and shares – and
presumably enough people seek it to make it financially
worthwhile offering the service. Every day, phone-in programmes on radio and TV feature astrologers whose opinions
are highly prized on deeply personal and potentially life-
changing decisions. Callers look to the stars and planets for
the solution to their problems of employment, relationships,
infertility, health and well-being. Nor is this concern for knowing the future restricted to the inadequate and the gullible.
Royalty and politicians also pay more than lip service to the
belief that the future can both be known and influenced by
tuning in to the right sources of cosmic information. Back in
1988, former White House chief of staff Donald T. Regan
claimed that the US president and his wife used an astrologer
to plan their lives. According to a report from Associated
Press dated 3 May 1988, it had been on such astrological
advice that President Ronald Reagan insisted on signing a
nuclear disarmament treaty with the Soviet leader Mikhail
Gorbachev some six months previously, at exactly 1.33 pm on
8 December 1987. Though the president himself denied mak-

ing policy decisions on such a basis, his wife's press secretary subsequently confirmed that she regularly consulted 'a friend that does astrology'. No one was surprised. After all, Reagan (like many US politicians) had been strongly influenced by fundamentalist groups who specialized in understanding the future. In a world where millions of us call astrological helplines to get detailed advice about the most intimate of relationships, and certain types of churches give credence to their own version of it, why should the president of the USA be any different?

Christians hold a variety of opinions on all this. Many smile, and think of it as a harmless pastime – unlikely to do much harm, even if it does no good. Others perceive the influence of dark, demonic forces behind it all. It is easy, for either reason, to dismiss people who seem more interested in the future than the present and regard them as, at best, escapists or, at worst, seriously maladjusted. But increasingly, those now talking of the end of the world as we know it in our generation are no longer members of fringe religious groups, nor are they unbalanced and insecure individuals who seek assurance about the future because they are incapable of coping with the present. Wherever we look – in government and in education as well as among ordinary citizens – there is a fresh awareness of the fact that as we approach the beginning of a new millennium this is the time to ask some serious questions about the future of the human race. Indeed, maybe this will be our last chance before chaos descends. For as the ruthless exploitation of the earth's resources continues unabated, and the gaps in the ozone layer expand annually, even scientists are getting concerned that we might yet be fried alive in our own lifetime as a result. At a more immediate level, many of the world's large conurbations are literally in danger of being buried beneath their own trash, while a rising tide of crime and violence threatens the safety and security of people all over the world, even in their own homes.

In their understandable eagerness to avoid being identified with some of the more bizarre doomsday sects, Christians should beware of not taking seriously enough these very real concerns. If the Christian Gospel is to be, as its name means, 'good news', then this is the time for a more profound engagement with the hopes and fears of this generation than we have hitherto known. That will not necessarily entail setting up our own millennial task forces to broadcast a 'Christian vision'. For Christians, sharing faith should always begin with recognizing their solidarity with other people. Time taken to reflect on where we are heading as we approach the end of the millennium will not be time wasted. On the contrary, it might enable us to hear what others are saying, and to empathize with the crisis that is moving relentlessly through our culture at this time.

When I was a child thirty years ago, in the middle of the social revolution of the 1960s, it seemed as if we had finally cracked it. If we didn't know the answers to all the world's questions, then at least we thought we knew where to look for them. The philosophical and practical foundations laid by the scientific and technological revolution in previous centuries had proved substantial enough to support a whole new concept of the world and of human nature and destiny, and we all took it for granted that the western values and lifestyles being affirmed then would be the ultimate and only answer to humanity's search for the good life. Today, all that is gone. As we move into the closing years of the 20th century, the frenzied search for a new world order grows in intensity almost daily. Not too many people support the old order any more – and this frustration and disillusionment is widespread not just among the popular media, but runs deep in most disciplines of the world of academic scholarship. Let me suggest three factors that are contributing to this surprising about-turn.

The year 2000 is coming up

This, of course, should be so obvious as hardly to be worth saying. But considering the fact that this is the 2000th anniversary of the birth of Jesus Christ, most Christians seem unbelievably casual about it. To call it a 'once-in-a-lifetime' opportunity is to belittle its enormous significance for the whole of the human race, and there are any number of organizations already moving into top gear as they plan their celebrations and marketing promotions for this unique point in time. As long ago as 1992, I attended a meeting to discuss the most effective ways for the mass media to mark the arrival of the new millennium. The occasion was chaired by an executive from a TV company, and included people from all walks of life in Scotland: education, industry, finance, commerce, as well as government. The person in the chair posed a simple question: 'Why is the year 2000 so special anyway? What is it that makes it worth celebrating?' The answers were interesting, if slightly predictable. A clear majority saw it as a chance to make a new start, to forget all the mess of the past century, turn over a new page in human history, and begin to construct the kind of world society we all profess to admire and long to enjoy. There was much idealistic talk of getting rid of injustice, poverty, famine, violence, abuse, and all the other things that have scarred so many people of our generation. But one thing surprised me. In all the discussion of the significance of the year 2000, not a single person mentioned – not even vaguely or in passing – the fact that these 2000 years are counted from the time when Jesus Christ was born. After something like forty minutes of brainstorming, I eventually threw this observation into the discussion. Predictably, perhaps, it was a conversation-stopper – at least for twenty or thirty seconds. Two things were obvious: first, that those present already knew that it would be the 2000th anniversary of the birth of Jesus. But even with the best will in the world these people (who were not anti-Christian, and some of them were church members) could not really see how that fact would have much relevance for the task of inspiring and equipping people for life in the new century. So where are the Christians? There are, of course, several Christian groups using the year 2000 as their focal point. But with one exception (the *Evangelization 2000* programme), they do not seem to be drawing attention to the distinctly Christian dimensions of that year – and if my experience is typical, none has penetrated the corridors of power in the mass media. Yet if so many people are looking at the year 2000 as the opportunity for a new beginning, when the mess of the past can somehow be cleaned up, is that not an open invitation for people of faith to share their distinctive vision for what the 21st century might become?

'Things can't go on like this for much longer – can they?'

No one should be surprised that the dawn of a new millennium might be a chance for humanity to make a new start. After all, most of us vow to do that on the first day of every new year! But the desire for fundamentally new directions for our culture runs much deeper than just the sentimentality and impermanence of a new year's resolution. Even serious academic thinkers are acknowledging that things cannot go on the way they are for much longer. There is a growing feeling that things are slipping away, the western world is in a crisis – and the condition is probably terminal. The philosophies that have guided and controlled our thinking for the last 500 years have run their course. The year 1992 was the 500th anniversary of Columbus's voyages of exploration, which took him and others out of their European homelands and to every corner of the planet. But it was scarcely celebrated, either in the old European homelands or in the 'new worlds' which were 'discovered' – and certainly not in the grand style that one might have anticipated. Sensitive and thinking people found themselves embarrassed and distressed by the long-term results of the great age of discovery and so-called enlightenment, and at best, the heritage of this 500-year period has become a liability from the past that no longer holds the power to inspire and give direction for the future.

In *Das Athanäum*, the eighteenth-century German diplomat Friedrich von Schlegel remarked that 'a historian is a prophet in reverse'. There is a lot of truth in that. Today was tomorrow yesterday, and being aware of our past can help us to be better equipped to deal with the present and the future. As we reflect on the crisis apparently gripping our civilization today, it is worth taking time to consider the roots of our culture. In a more profound way than we often realize, modern western thinking does indeed go back to the days of Columbus and his contemporaries. Excited by their discoveries of 'new' lands, sixteenth-century European visionaries soon began to wonder what other unknown horizons were waiting to be explored. A new age of scientific investigation was about to dawn. Within a very short time, there was a veritable explosion of new knowledge that soon encompassed the whole range of human experience – and changed our understanding of ourselves and the world for good. Copernicus (1473–1543) challenged the old idea that the earth was the centre of the universe, and convincingly demonstrated that the sun was the centre, and when the Italian astronomer Galileo (1564–1642) popularized the idea, he soon found himself on a collision course with the Establishment. But in due course the new idea was accepted, and an alternative view that had prevailed since ancient times was discarded. There was a paradigm shift of massive dimensions, that merely served to give permission to others to ask further questions, not only about science but about human nature.

In the middle of the 17th century, Sir Isaac Newton wondered why apples always fall downwards and not up – and came up with the law of gravity to explain it. His notion that everything worked according to carefully defined and unchanging laws of nature heralded another paradigm shift, as people came to think of the universe as a gigantic machine. Science and technology were born and, with the Industrial Revolution, such discoveries were put to creative use for the benefit of ordinary people. No wonder that this period of history soon came to be referred to as 'the Enlightenment'. For that is just what it seemed to be. Compared with what was now being discovered, the old world of the Middle Ages and the ancients was nothing but darkness – full of superstition and ignorance. Before, people had believed their lives to be hemmed in by cosmic forces beyond both their control and their understanding. Now, new possibilities seemed to stretch out endlessly, and the only limit to progress would be human ingenuity. There were still many uncertainties, but for the first time in the whole of human history it looked as if people would be able to control their environment, rather than the environment controlling them. Great voyages of discovery became commonplace, and with them the imperialistic expansion of Britain and other western powers into virtually every part of the globe. These were heady days, when it seemed that human endeavour could achieve just about anything.

Today, of course, all that has been swept away. The old certainties of the Enlightenment are no longer secure, and science and technology have failed to deliver the goods. In the 20th century, the very things that were supposed to bring progress have often led us to the brink of destruction, and in the process have inhibited and devalued significant areas of human experience and understanding. No one would wish to turn the clock back, nor to deny the usefulness of the advances in human knowledge there have been in the last two or three centuries. There has been tremendous progress, and much of it has been enormously beneficial to the entire human race. But it is also undeniable that when we look more closely at this golden coin of modern progress, more often than not the flip side is heavily tarnished.

A hundred years ago, the invention of the internal combustion engine was beginning to revolutionize daily life. It was unquestionably a great discovery, and has made life easier for all succeeding generations. But it has not all been good news, and the very machines that make modern transportation so efficient are in danger of destroying both our social environment and, ultimately perhaps, the planet itself. Or consider modern agriculture, where artificial pesticides and fertilizers enable us to grow food crops with predictable regularity, so that every vegetable in every supermarket throughout the western world can be guaranteed to be of a particular shape, size, colour and quality. If that seems a dubious advantage, then remember that, though too many are still starving, such technology has enabled us to feed far more people than our ancestors could ever have believed possible. Yet in many places, the same fertilizers and pesticides that have had such generally beneficial effects have also poisoned the most basic human food resource of all, namely the water supply. Or think of medical science. None of us would wish to go back to the days before the discovery of anaesthetics and antibiotics. But conventional western medicine often treats patients as if they are no more than dead bodies that happen to be still breathing. People are seen as machines, and illness is defined as malfunction of the parts. Doctors restore 'health' by tinkering with the defective organs to make them work properly. There is nothing at all wrong with that, except that it is only half the picture. Most people do not think of themselves as machines, and they instinctively know that having a perfectly functioning body does not automatically produce wholeness and well-being. People are not just bundles of spare parts, but have emotions and relationships that have their own crucial part to play in ensuring human satisfaction. It is taking traditional western medics a long time to accept this, and in the meantime many look to complementary therapists of various kinds who seem better equipped to take account of the more personal and spiritual aspects of wholeness.

On his return from the Soviet Union in 1919, the US jour-
nalist Lincoln Steffens reported, 'I have seen the future and it
works.'[1] That sentiment would not be shared by many people
today. As we approach the dawn of a new millennium, there is
a sense in which we have already seen the future, and we
know it *doesn't* work – and we want to make radical changes
before it's too late. Moreover, these changes need to be more
than cosmetic. It is not just that the Enlightenment vision has
become dimmed, but that the foundational concepts on which
the Enlightenment was based are themselves part of the problem. Think for a moment of three of the key philosophical
notions on which western culture has been founded. There
was 'rationalism', the idea that the only things worth knowing
are things you can think about. There is nothing wrong with
thinking, of course, but the way we have tended to major on
this to the exclusion of all else has left millions of western
people emotionally powerless. Then there was also 'materialism', the belief that the only things worth thinking about are
what you can see and touch – an attitude that has cut us adrift
from any sense of spiritual moorings. And then 'reductionism',
the idea that you understand things by taking them to pieces –
a procedure that has led, amongst other things, to personal
alienation, and is at the root of much of the destruction of our
natural environment. No wonder that many see our culture in
terminal crisis. The vision that inspired the past can never
provide answers for the future, because it is itself part of the
problem. Somewhere along the line, something significant has
been lost – a sense of our own humanity, values, and spirituality.

'More spirituality and less materialism'

You might be forgiven for thinking this would be the phrase of
a religious leader. But you would be wrong. It was not a bishop
or other Christian leader who used it. It comes from the autobiography of British actress Joanna Lumley, who goes on to
say, 'In the 1990s we're going to start finding our souls again.
We've gone through a very non-spiritual time this century.'[2] A
recent issue of the youth magazine of the British TSB bank
put it this way: 'After the 60s and Hippies, after the 70s and
Rock 'n' Roll drugs, after the 80s and post-mod radical chic
OK Yah materialism, after everything ... there's a more spiritual way to guide us through to the 90s and beyond.'[3] Smile at
the journalistic hype if you please, but remember that these
are not the words of some cranky religious cult leader.
Financial institutions are an entrenched part of the western
Establishment, and when the Establishment speaks in this
way you can be sure there is a growing conviction that we
need spiritual answers to some of the apparently intractable
problems which we now face. In more reflective – but no less
committed – vein, American psychology professor Marilyn
Ferguson wrote as long ago as 1980 that 'the entire culture is
undergoing trauma and tensions that beg for new order'.[4]

You might suppose this renewed awareness of the spiritual
is good news for Christians. But the exact opposite is the case.
The western Church is actually in a weak position, for the very
simple reason that to most people it is a part of the same insti-
tutionalized authority structure that helped create the mess in
the first place. Among the leaders of today's generation, there
is an insistent and growing belief that Christianity is irrelevant. Modern western thinking, it is said, has largely been
dominated by Christian values, and these must therefore have

contributed to our present predicament. That being the case, it stands to reason that we will not solve things by doing more of the same. It can be debated whether Christian values shaped the Enlightenment, or whether it was the other way round, and the Church has allowed itself to be taken over by essentially secular values.[5] Either way, the practical outcome is no different: Christianity is very firmly perceived as part of the old order, and therefore something to be discarded rather than trusted for the future.[6] As a result, people searching for a spiritual dimension to life today are unlikely to have much expectation of finding it in the Church. In medical circles, for instance, there is a concerted effort to identify ways of including 'spirituality' within the healing process, but it is generally taken for granted that, whatever 'spirituality' is (and there is a good deal of uncertainty over that), it has nothing at all to do with the work of hospital chaplains and organized religion. They are all seen as part of a system that has failed us, and the way forward will be in our exploration of and openness to alternative ways of ordering things and understanding the world.

This explains why there is so much interest today in other cultures. If, as is claimed, we need to rediscover spirituality in order to put things right, and if (as is also believed) the traditional sources of spiritual wisdom in the west (the churches) have dried up, then there is nowhere else to look but to other cultures and worldviews, or within ourselves. For some, this takes the form of studying major non-western thought systems such as the great religions of the orient. For others, it means a concern to rediscover and preserve the native cultures that were displaced when white people first invaded the Americas, Australasia or Africa. Yet others see the solution in a kind of reversal of history, by jumping backwards over the last thousand years or more into the dim and distant pre-Christian past of Europe itself, to embrace and affirm the long-lost values and worldviews of our own pagan ancestors. As a result, a dazzling and bewildering array of different spiritualities compete for attention, each of them claiming to be able to offer something that will help us find our souls again, and chart a safe course for the future. The goods on offer in this religious market-place range from messages from spirit guides and extraterrestrials, to neo-paganism, celtic mythology and aboriginal spirituality – not to mention renewed interest in astrology and a vast range of psychological therapies offering the prospect of a renewed, holistic humanity.

Back in the middle of the first century, the Roman satirist Petronius observed that 'the gods walk abroad so commonly in our streets that it is easier to meet a god than a man'.[7] The same thing could be said of many cities in the west today. History is coming full circle. The complacency of Christians in this situation both amazes and horrifies me. For people who should be operating at the cutting edge of our culture, far too many Christian leaders seem almost totally unaware of this enormous spiritual movement of our day. Yet most of my junk mail relates to it, in one way or another! Even those who are aware rarely engage with this spiritual search in any constructive or serious way. It is easy to dismiss all this by sticking labels onto it. To call it the 'New Age Movement' makes it sound like the work of a minority pressure group that sooner or later will disappear. There is undoubtedly a great deal of movement and change around today, and the present spiritual search is by any definition an eclectic phenomenon that is in a state of constant flux. But it is not a movement in the sense of being a passing fad. Without question, this is the shape of things to come, and when the people of 2020 look back to the 1980s and 1990s, I believe they will see that we have been in the middle of a paradigm shift as significant as those inaugurated in the past by Copernicus, Newton or Einstein.

Wherever we look, from industry to the home, our institutions are collapsing – including, above all, the traditional western spiritual institutions (the churches). At a time when traditional answers no longer seem to make sense, it is inevitable that sensitive and thinking people will turn to other things. Even so, the spiritual about-turn has been dramatic. Just twenty years ago, a rationalist-materialist worldview still dominated the lives of most people – and precluded the possibility of belief in any sort of mystical or spiritual dimension to life (whether Christian or otherwise). Today, it is no problem to find practising shamans in the main streets of western cities, while statistics show that in the former West Germany alone there were something like 90,000 registered witches and wizards.[8] Europe is poised on a knife-edge, and may be entering a new socially-regressive dark age not only with the rise of ethnic strife, but also the re-emergence of neo-Nazi movements. Given the close connections of Hitler himself with spiritistic practices, it is difficult to resist the conclusion that these two forces go hand in hand.[9]

This whole phenomenon is both the greatest single threat to Christianity in the west, and also its greatest single opportunity for many decades. There is a tremendous – and growing – interest in the supernatural, the mystical and the spiritual among younger people in particular. Western governments struggle to encourage more school-leavers to take up careers in science and technology. But there is a strong tide running

in the opposite direction, and universities in many countries
are faced with the unexpected phenomenon of massive growth
in the numbers of students wanting to study religion. After
300 years of dominance, the Enlightenment values are crum-
bling fast, for very few of today's students are rationalists or
materialists of the kind that were commonplace even a decade
ago. Not long ago, I gave an address in one of Britain's most
ancient universities. It was about the so-called 'New Age' phenomenon, and after I spoke the person chairing the meeting
(which was part of a Christian mission) asked for questions
and comments. A man in his forties jumped up right away: 'I
am a professor of chemical engineering,' he said, 'but I've
been a wizard for the last fifteen years, and I'm thinking of
becoming a Christian.' The chairperson was lost for words!
The combination of being a university professor, a wizard and
a potential convert to Christianity was simply mind-blowing.
But in the course of further conversation, I discovered it was
all true. In his professional life, this man was a successful science professor, but at home he lived like a medieval
alchemist. His apartment was full of magical potions, books of
spells, sacred bones and feathers – even a witch's broomstick.
Yet he wanted to be a Christian! What then transpired was
like a scene from the New Testament as he took all this para-
phernalia outside and burned it. That episode encapsulates
the evangelistic opportunity that is presented to the Church
today. Here was an intelligent, educated person, a leader in
society, who spent his spare time in magic and spiritistic practices, and yet was more than open to Christian faith once he
knew what it was about. But when he stood up and made that
statement in public, the Christians who were there all disappeared into the woodwork as fast as they could make it! It is

difficult to know whether to be more alarmed by the nature of the spirituality rising in our culture, or the apparent inability of most Christians either to understand or relate to it.

CHALLENGES FOR THE CHURCH

The picture so far has been sketched out using broad brush strokes. Now we need to be a little more specific. Where exactly are we heading, as we move ever closer to the new millennium? It is impossible – and unwise – to make detailed predictions, and maybe only one thing is certain anyway: wherever our destination, we are definitely going there in the fast track. Change in a very big way is the name of the game, and whereas in the past changes took decades to filter through, today's new idea is often superseded even before it has a chance to establish itself. This presents new challenges, especially for institutions like the Church. At one time, society could move slowly, accommodating change gradually by making small adjustments as one generation succeeded another. In that climate, it was possible for the Church to catch up gradually with the culture in which it had to minister. Today, that is no longer possible. Any institution that is not at the cutting edge of change is soon going to find itself cast on one side as irrelevant and unhelpful, no matter how grandiose its claims to truth may be. 'The more the rate of change increases, the more the problems that face us change and the shorter is the life of the solutions we find to them. Therefore, by the time we find solutions to many of the problems that face us, usually the most important ones, the problems have so changed that our solutions to them are no longer relevant or effective ... In other words, many of our solutions are to problems that no longer exist in the form in which they were solved. As a result we are falling further and further behind our times.'[10] That was written back in 1981 about secular business organizations, though its appropriateness to the Church is obvious. Since then, cultural change has accelerated fast, and the challenge will only intensify as the new millennium approaches.

What are the needs of the world to which the Church should respond in order to minister effectively to people of the 21st century? The search for a new worldview that can provide a credible ideological foundation for western culture is obviously fundamental, and we will keep returning to that theme throughout this book. But in terms of everyday life, changing assumptions and values generally take a different, more personal form. Simone Weil once wrote that 'the future is made of the same stuff as the present',[11] and some of today's significant issues will undoubtedly dominate the agenda for the foreseeable future – though we must always expect the unexpected, even if we cannot plan for it.

Political and Economic Changes

The world is not the same today as it was forty years ago. Europeans need look no further than their own continent for proof of that. In both east and west, Europe has little clear sense of either identity or purpose. Who would have believed in 1980 that communism would be in a state of terminal decline only ten years later? The steady forward march of this totalitarian system seemed set to continue without visible end, dominating not only its traditional strongholds in eastern

Europe, but extending its influence into many countries of the developing world. Even with the insights of someone as skilful as Mikhail Gorbachev, the communist system proved to be incapable of effective reform. In its European version it is now a thing of the past – though westerners should be reminded that (so far) it has managed to survive elsewhere, including China which is the world's most populous nation. The fall of the Berlin Wall and the disappearance of other obvious physical signs of communist oppression was greeted with euphoria in western European capitals, but the demise of the communist system has not given birth to the democratic, capitalist utopia confidently predicted for so long by its enemies. In many previously communist states, one form of exploitation and state-inspired terrorism has merely given way to another, as ethnic tension and violence have again risen to the surface of European politics. Ancient animosities that seemed long-since dead have been resurrected, and the brutality with which rival armies have opposed one another in places like Bosnia has rivalled even Hitler's Germany for savagery and inhumanity.

The countries of western Europe have, in general, escaped the worst horrors of this social turmoil, but the European Community wrestles with its own problems. Back in the 1970s, its creators believed it could be the solution to all of Europe's problems. Today, that hope seems, at best, impossibly optimistic. Economic, social and political co-operation, let alone union, are little more than elusive shadows, and the inability of the Community even to form a common foreign policy in relation to the tragic events being played out on its own eastern borders only serves to highlight a major failure of nerve, and identifies a bigger and more disturbing question.

What exactly is 'Europe'? In what sense is Europe an identifiable place? Is it even a geographical unit – or are these countries bound together only by the fact that for centuries their histories have impinged on one another? Could it be that the idea of 'Europe' as a unified concept had its origins not in geography or ethnicity, but in religion and ideology? Was 'Europe' a notion that only made sense as long as Christianity was the binding force holding these otherwise disparate nations together, giving them a common worldview and set of values? Is it going too far to wonder if a Europe bereft of its Christian foundations can ever be a cultural unity at all? Will Europe in the 21st century revert to being what it physically is, just an appendage to Asia?

Things are no more clear-cut in that other superpower of the 20th century, the USA. Following the Second World War, American values and national identity were largely shaped by the perceived threat to world peace coming from the old Soviet Union and its satellite states around the world. Despite all the rhetoric about upholding traditional American standards, what President Ronald Reagan once dubbed the 'evil empire' was in effect calling many of the shots in US policy, domestic as well as foreign. The demise of the Soviet Union has forced the USA onto the defensive in trying to redefine its role and identity in the new world order. In an interview with the *Washington Post* on 15 October 1993, President Bill Clinton admitted, 'I even made a crack the other day. I said, "Gosh, I miss the cold war"...'[12] Moreover, the USA faces the same kind of internal ambiguities as the Europeans. Who exactly are the Americans? That might sound like a silly question, but it was at the heart of the nation's ambivalence about celebrating the 500th anniversary of Columbus's voyages of exploration to the so-called 'new world'. To those who already lived there, it never was the 'new world' – and so the USA is still struggling with profound questions about its own national identity. Though the reins of power and influence are largely held by people from a Caucasian background, there are other significant groups with at least as much right (if not, in some cases, more) to be regarded as 'real' Americans. This great country is an amalgam of native Americans, African Americans, Asian Americans, Hispanic Americans, as well as Caucasians, all living together in what, in cultural terms, is a somewhat uneasy truce that needs little provocation before the cracks begin to show.

While Europeans and Americans are looking within to patch up their failing vision, the whole world centre of gravity is moving elsewhere. The economic power of the west has been in decline for the last forty years or more, but because of the inherited wealth and traditions of the preceding 500 years, it was possible for westerners still to behave as if they were truly in control of things. That is no longer the case. The majority of the world's people have always lived in the two-thirds world. Today, they are getting influence commensurate with their numbers, and many of the most significant decision-making and trend-setting processes have moved east. The Pacific Rim is now the world's economic powerhouse, and we can expect other parts of the two-thirds world increasingly to take responsibility for setting the agenda in the next century and beyond.

The influence of the two-thirds world will not just be economic, for alongside the economic growth there are some significant religious and social factors. Everyone knows about the rise of so-called Fundamentalist Islam. At least, everyone knows what the western media – who are generally militantly anti-Muslim – report of it.[13] Yet clearly, Islamic values are not as alien to western people as the media would have us believe. How, otherwise, can the growth of Islam in the west be explained, especially when many of the converts are white, western people with no ethnic or other ties to traditionally Islamic nations? Such converts are clearly affirming the positive usefulness of Islamic values as they attempt to make sense out of the jumble that is modern western culture.[14] Christians who become paranoid about the growth of Islam in the west are often uncritically accepting the distorted (and, arguably, racist) media view of this ancient faith. The fact is that there are still far more Christians in the world than there are adherents of any other faith – almost two billion of them. At a time when an average of 7,500 people leave the Church every day in Europe alone,[15] there is no denying that Christianity is disintegrating in the west, though there is no evidence that this is in any way linked with or leading to a significant expansion of Islam. On the contrary, there is every reason to believe that the failure of the Church is more closely paralleled by the rise in popularity of New Age spirituality. In world terms, talk of Christianity in decline is absurd. One of the ironies of our time is that as westerners question and reject Christianity, the ever-increasing populations of the two-thirds world are embracing Christian faith in vast numbers. Some 60 per cent of all the world's Christians now live in the developing world, and are not white westerners. Though there is still a significant Christian missionary enterprise, it is rapidly moving into reverse gear as Christian missionaries are now travelling from places like Africa and South America to share their faith in the traditional Christian heartlands of

Europe, North America and Australasia.[16] In parallel with the shift in the world's economic centre of gravity from the west to the Pacific, there is another great shift in the centre of gravity of Christian faith. For its first thousand years, Christianity was the faith of the Mediterranean lands where it originated. During its second thousand years, it was the faith of people in Europe and the lands to which they emigrated, predominantly North America and Australasia. At the beginning of its third millennium, Christianity is without question the faith of the people of the two-thirds world. Western Christians who wish to take their evangelistic calling seriously will need to take account of the fact that the majority of the world's Christians are no longer like them. While the western churches decline, Christianity elsewhere is expanding very fast. There must be lessons to be learned from this which can benefit the western Church, but it will be a painful process for westerners to learn how to accept new insights from those who have all too often been regarded as spiritually inferior and unsophisticated.

Lifestyle Changes

If anything, the pace of change in western lifestyles is even faster than in other areas we have mentioned here. As a result of new opportunities for worldwide travel, people are becoming more aware of different cultures than their own. This is having a profound effect on what we eat, the kind of medicine we practise, and the ways in which we expect to make sense out of life. We now know that Christianity is not the only possible religious faith, and there is growing admiration for the achievements of other cultures as people discover that for the past few centuries it is the west that has been the aberration,

not the rest of the world. For while westerners confidently supposed that religion was dead, most of the world's people continued to find meaning and significance through religious
faith. Coupled with a genuine search for personal identity,
meaning and purpose in life, appreciating that has encouraged
people in the west to adopt a much more open-ended
approach in their search for personal fulfilment.

The information and communication revolution has also
changed the outlook of most people. It is now possible to
access data files all across the world using a personal computer and a phone line. Of course, the accessibility of so much
information raises new questions, not least how to find enough
time to process and use it all. But the problems raised for the
Church by what is essentially a non-book culture are enormous. The growth in the entertainment and leisure industries
has the same impact. Even in my lifetime we have gone from
cracked gramophone record to compact disc and interactive
video. There are so many options now open to us for our
leisure that people are even stressed making decisions about
how to enjoy themselves. In fact, the nature of leisure itself is
changing, as people seek to define their identity through what
they do in their own personal time rather than what they do in
paid employment. We will not be far into the 21st century
before it will be the norm for people to design their own
lifestyle portfolio of part-time work, voluntary service, and
self-expressive leisure activities – partly because of increasing concern about the quality of life, but also because changing patterns of business organization are providing fewer and
fewer full-time job opportunities.[17] In this climate, church-
going and religious involvement will inevitably be sidelined
unless they appear to offer the promise of something that is

worth giving one's time and talents for. The major challenge for evangelism will be how to reach the person who says they can live quite well without God.

Family structures are also changing rapidly, and while many agree that a major cause of social suffering today is the disintegration of the traditional family, there is no consensus about what can be put in its place. Single-parent families, blended families, multi-generational households, even street gangs, are the norm for many of today's children. Some children literally have no idea who their real parents are, as partners remarry, divorce and cohabit with increasing speed. The dysfunctional family is widespread, with abuse and violence found at all levels of society. Then there is the fact that cohabitation is increasingly favoured in preference to marriage, at least on a short-term basis, while recent figures suggest that one in four of all mothers over forty in the UK are now unmarried, by choice.[18] Is this a genuine change in our culture? It is certainly symptomatic of a real search for new ways of community — but have Christians taken it all seriously enough to be able to have something useful to say?

This then is the confusing, yet dynamic jungle that we live in as we approach the end of the millennium. This is where today's Christians are called to be salt and light, sharing the good news of which Jesus spoke. What does it all mean, and how can the Church respond in ways that will be culturally appropriate, while still reflecting the ultimate values of the Gospel? These are big questions, and we will be doing well if we can even set up a few signposts by the end of this book. As we seek new vision and empowerment for the task, I am reminded of a story told by Australian sociologists Peter and Sue Kaldor:[19]

Once upon a time there was a mighty river. It flowed gracefully and elegantly across the landscape. Along its banks it gave life and sustenance to the tribes of Aboriginal Australians who camped by it. For many generations this river was a central focus for life. Then, gradually, the river ceased to flow, becoming a stagnant pool. With the heat of summer it started to dry up. Around the banks of the disappearing symbol of their security, the people watched aghast. What could be happening to them? By the dried-up riverbed many sat, waiting for the river to flow once more.

Yet others thought to look around and discovered that the river was not gone. Still flowing, it had simply changed course upstream, creating a billabong on the curve at which they sat.

Most Christians in the west can see that things have changed, and the world has moved on. But too many are still sitting by the dried-up riverbed, hoping the water will flow back the way it once did. It takes neither faith nor courage to do that. It is more demanding to step out and take risks, to experiment in order to discover where God's life-giving Spirit is moving in today's world. To move away might mean the dismantling of our institutions, the sacrifice of some sacred cows – and that is always painful. But if the experience of the world Church is anything to go by, it might also mean a rediscovery of the Gospel and some exciting surprises. Whatever the cost, this could be where God is calling the Church to go. For the size of the opportunity more than matches the dimensions of the chal-

lenge: 'The future of humanity could easily be more depen-
dent on our moving with this moment of grace than on anything else being done in the world today. If we truly believe
that Jesus is the God-sent answer to our human needs but fail
to share that answer with others, the next millennium could
become the last.'[20]

chapter two | Where do We go from Here?

The European Enlightenment has had a profound and far-reaching impact on Christian thinking. To a much greater extent than many Christians care to admit, the Church has been dominated by the ideological values of our essentially secular culture. As a result, Christians have taken it for granted that faith is a matter of private opinion, with no direct relevance to the real world of politics, or science, or economics. They have accepted the basic rationalist understanding of how things might be known, and what is worth knowing. They have promoted a materialist attitude to the mystical and the numinous, and theological scholarship and education has applied a reductionist methodology of understanding things in a more thoroughgoing way than almost any other intellectual discipline.[1]

When some contemporary critics of Christianity claim that the Church has become so hopelessly identified with the problems in our culture that it has no useful contribution to the search for new solutions, they frequently exaggerate and overstate their case.[2] But that is not to say that their analysis is completely wrong, and the only Christian response should be one of rejection and retrenchment. Today's Christians are heirs to the past, and as Christians face up to the challenge of the re-evangelization of the west, they will need to own some of the baggage from that past. A revisionist version of Christian history will be seen for what it is: a whitewashing of past mistakes, and an attempt to avoid any sense of shared responsibility for them.

Of course, we need to get all this into perspective. Some scholars today write as if the Enlightenment was the greatest disaster ever to befall the human race. We all know that is not true. Despite the current emphasis on holistic healthcare, for example, nobody would really want to turn the clock back to the medical practices of 200 years ago, nor to return to the way things were before the invention of mass transportation systems. The Enlightenment and its values are not all bad news, and in our eagerness to distance ourselves from some of the mistaken excesses of the past, it does no harm for us to be reminded of the positive side. Take, for example, the emphasis on reason, and the consequent insistence that faith needs to have a rational foundation. A couple of generations ago that led to the conclusion that, in religious terms, nothing could possibly be worth believing. With the questioning of that outlook, much contemporary speculation on spirituality seems to have swung to the opposite extreme, and we now live in a culture where everything and anything seems to be worth believing, and for some people the more bizarre and unlikely it is on the rational level, then the more value there is in believing it. Bearing witness to faith in a generation that is increasingly attracted to the irrational as an alternative to materialist rationalism might need to begin by underlining the importance of thinking. Being rational about things is not necessarily the same as being a rationalist – nor for that matter is irrationality the only alternative to an over-confident rationalism. There is more to the human personality than a left-brained analytical understanding of things, and the non-rational or right-brained side of ourselves, as experienced and expressed through the emotions and intuitions, is undoubtedly more important than western people have typically allowed.[3] But if we depend only on our non-rational intuitions it is all too easy to misrepresent and misunderstand things in a way that will effectively undermine any serious spiritual search for truth. Writing about her own mystical spirituality, Shirley Maclaine says that 'It seems to be all about feeling, not thinking'.[4] Bhagwan Shree Rajneesh went further, and insisted that 'It is not that the intellect sometimes misunderstands. It is not that the intellect sometimes errs; it is that the intellect is the error.'[5]

That kind of attitude is widespread, and is creating problems in many different fields of intellectual endeavour. The history and culture of ancient Celts are being rewritten as modern spiritual searchers hunt for something amenable to their own perceptions, while the same mindset is encouraging others to ransack indiscriminately the great religions of the east in the search for spiritual goodies that will suit the current religious appetites of the west.[6] As part of the same process, the history of Christianity is regularly rewritten and misunderstood, while Christian belief is misrepresented. For example, it is widely taken for granted that, if there is such a person as the 'real Jesus', he is not to be found in the pages of the New Testament but in esoteric Gnostic gospels that circulated on the fringes of Christianity in the third and fourth centuries and were allegedly repressed by early church leaders for essentially political reasons. Nor is there any shortage of people who will claim (against all the historical evidence) that the canon of the Bible itself was concocted in the 4th century by nasty male chauvinists, whose main concern was to put women down and to disinfect its contents so as to remove notions like reincarnation, which allegedly were there in the beginning, but became an embarrassing inconvenience to the Church's political philosophy.[7]

Unfortunately, Christians sometimes do the same thing. I remember a sermon on the story of how Peter walked on the water to meet Jesus (Matthew 14:22–33). The preacher began by saying, 'I'm an old-fashioned fundamentalist – I believe it', and then proceeded to expound the Bible text by claiming that only Peter was brave enough to try walking on water, because James and John were landlubbers who hated the sea. The New Testament, of course, gives no basis whatever for this view. On the contrary, it insists that all three of them were fishermen. But that made no difference to this particular preacher because he 'felt' that must have been how it was. As a result, the indisputable facts of the New Testament story were suppressed in favour of what he wanted to say about modern Christian discipleship. As it happened, his message was otherwise unexceptionable, and one could argue that no real harm was done – except that his youthful audience were given the impression that it is all right to play fast and loose with the Bible. In the hands of others, however, the same approach to rationality can lead to a redefinition of the Bible's message that has more serious consequences. The purveyors of the so-called 'prosperity gospel' adopt exactly the same attitudes, with their easy insistence that following Jesus ensures health, wealth and long life – and the consequent conclusion that anyone not enjoying these benefits is somehow not fully obedient to the Gospel.[8] Many people today seem unable to tell the difference between fact and fantasy, and bearing witness to the

Gospel in our generation might need to begin with an insistence that there are at least *some* objective realities out there! The critical attitude engendered by the Enlightenment emphasis on reason is far from being all bad news!

At the same time, no one can deny that to be of maximum effectiveness, Christians will need to change. Wherever we look, churches seem to be agonizing over this question today. Will they change? Why should they change? Can they afford to change? And what changes are worth making anyway? This is not the most useful way to phrase the question. The fact is that, whether we recognize it or not, we are all changing all the time. The real choice for Christians is whether they allow the world to change them (and it will – in accordance with its own standards and values), or whether they will take the initiative to become the God-driven force that changes the world. Several areas in particular require some urgent attention and creative thinking. In this chapter we shall survey them at the grand, visionary level, reserving a more detailed unpacking for later chapters.

THE BIBLE

All over the world today the Bible is close to the heartbeat of fast-growing churches. As ordinary people – often newly-literate people – come face to face with its message, they find themselves propelled in life-changing new directions that influence not just personal religious beliefs but, in many places, the whole political and social structure.[9] By contrast, in the Christian heartlands of Europe, the Bible has been consistently studied and preached for 500 years or more – and it seems to have exactly the opposite effect. Instead of being inspired to passionate fervour by its message, people appear to be turned off by it – and that goes for church members just as much as for non-Christians. Why? This is an urgent question for western Christians, and there are many legitimate ways of addressing it. It will surface in several forms in the course of this book. A basic part of the challenge is how to relate the Bible to other aspects of people's normal life experience. This comes from two directions: how can we read the Bible, and how can we relate our own experience of faith to what we find in it, in such a way that on the basis of our understandings we can then stimulate and facilitate other people's faith pilgrimages?

The diagram illustrates clearly enough where much – if not most – contemporary Bible exposition begins. On the one hand, there are the issues and questions of contemporary society. Of course, these things usually present themselves in specific contexts, as the problems of particular people in particular times and places. The received wisdom encourages the reader to reason from the particular to the universal, and then attempt to tackle broad, general principles rather than the specific examples we all face day by day. But how can we bring the Bible alongside these abstracted principles, when it also is mostly a book full of stories? Inevitably, we go through the same process with the Bible, cutting through the stories to extrapolate from them a collection of notions that can be labelled 'biblical principles'. The interpreter then tries to bring these 'biblical principles' alongside the issues we perceive to be the problem in real life, and hopefully the one will be able to inform and address the other – while all the time, the Bible readers themselves stand in splendid isolation from this whole procedure, as if playing a game by remote control. This is the classic Enlightenment-inspired reductionist hermeneutic embodied in the historical-critical methodology that for generations has dominated western theological education.[10] It leaves no space for the interaction of personal faith stories with the Bible stories (that would be 'subjective') nor, in the hands of most of its exponents, does it leave any space for the intrusion of the spiritual or the mystical (that would be to allow non-scientific assumptions to violate the supposed 'objectivity' of the interpretative process).

For people trained in this way of understanding, it can be quite a shock to discover that this is not how the majority of the world's Christians typically read the Bible. I remember

visiting with a group of Christians living on Smokey Mountain, a huge garbage tip in Manila in the Philippines. It was about as challenging an experience as any white Anglo-Saxon Protestant male could ever have. For one thing, I must have been the oldest person there. Unlike the churches in the west, Christian groups elsewhere are not predominantly made up of older people, but of the young – partly reflecting the population balance in most developing countries (just over 40 per cent of the population of the Philippines is under fifteen years old). This particular group was led by a young woman who must certainly have been in her mid-teens. The only bits of the Bible they had were a few scraps (probably rescued from the tip) which she proceeded to read. She read in English, for my benefit, and as she did so I at least felt at home with the Bible story to which she drew our attention. It was Jesus' parable of the Good Samaritan (Luke 10:29–37). I could see it was new for several of them, though to me it was a familiar story. I thought I knew all there was to know about it, and when the group leader asked the question, 'Now who are you in this story?' I took it for granted that I knew the answer to that as well. At least, I knew who I would like to be. That was easy. I recognized the possibility that I might be the priest or the Levite, who passed by the wounded man and left him on the roadside. I knew I would really like to be the Samaritan, who did good by taking the robbers' victim to a place of safety – though in my heart of hearts I had the sneaking suspicion that (in common with many western people) maybe I was more like the innkeeper, who would do good but only when someone else paid him for it. Anyway, when we were given the opportunity to share our thoughts with one another, I had no difficulty knowing what I was going to say. It was just as well that I was not invited to speak first, for I soon realized that I was responding quite differently from everyone else who was there. For them, there were no agonizing choices as they sought to identify with the characters in the story. They all knew precisely who they were: the person beaten up and left for dead by the roadside. I realized in an instant what was happening. Though I had debated within myself who I might be, in reality my options were strictly limited because I had taken it for granted that, whoever I was, I would be one of the authority figures in this story. It simply never occurred to me that I might be poor and powerless like the man on the roadside. As I realized what I had done, I could hardly believe it. I thought of myself as globally aware and politically correct – yet, even surrounded by the sights and smells of such obvious poverty, I still unconsciously read into this Bible story the imperialistic assumptions of my culture, assuming that if I was in there at all, then I would have to be in control of somebody.

Poor people in the two-thirds world are not the only ones who look at the Bible in a different way from traditional western Christians. People in our own culture also have a lot of challenging questions, and we do not always know how to use the Bible in addressing them. I remember being invited to give one of the keynote addresses at a large Christian teaching event in the UK. My subject was to be Abraham – and I had a pretty good idea what the organizers wanted me to say about him. Was he not a man of great faith, the founder of the people of God, and commended in the New Testament as a role model for Christian believers? Of course. But as I read his story more closely in the light of the realities of life in Britain today, that all seemed a million miles away. For Abraham was also a man who without hesitation encouraged the king of Egypt to have

sex with his wife Sarah, when he thought it would save his
own skin (Genesis 12:10–20). He was a man who chose another sexual partner when the same Sarah failed to deliver him a
son (Genesis 16:1–4). He was a man who, when Sarah eventually did have a child, deliberately engineered tensions
between his two partners and their sons (Genesis 21:8–14),
and who generally engaged in domestic abuse and violence of
a most horrific sort. Reading the Bible twenty years ago, I
don't suppose I would have noticed much of that. But in
today's world, these are key issues. If this is the kind of role
model the Bible gives us, then who needs the Bible? As I
struggled with this particular passage, one of the few things
that was completely clear to me was that a historical-critical
exegesis of the passage was unlikely to yield many answers.[11]
What I needed was a more intuitive understanding of the tensions in Abraham's family – and of how God somehow could
be found in the middle of so much exploitation and suffering.
My partner Olive has an extensive ministry in the creative
arts, and at the time she happened to be doing a lot of work
with mask-making as an aid to the exploration of personal
spirituality. To cut a long story short, I made a series of masks
of the various characters who feature in the Abraham story,
first imagining and then reproducing in plaster on my own
face the expressions of Sarah, Hagar, Ishmael, Isaac – and
Abraham – as at different points in the story they came to
terms with the dynamics of their home life and relationships.[12]
The result was stunning. Abraham genuinely wanted to serve
God – there was no doubt of that. But his faith was so self-
centred that he was incapable of seeing what he was doing to
those around him. And the good news was that, far from being
a model of morality to be followed by today's Christians,

Abraham's imperfections were a mirror in which we could see our own struggles, and discern God's loving presence even in all this mess — as the God of Abraham actually turned out to be on the side of those whom he abused and victimized.[13] As I delivered that address I was well aware that I was looking at this familiar story not only from a different angle, but in a way that could be potentially disturbing for some of my hearers. I need not have worried, for Christians with similar life stories (violent people like Abraham, as well as his victims) came cautiously out of the woodwork to claim the healing which the Bible also seemed to offer them. The recording of that talk has been used around the world, and the same result has always followed.

Now what was I doing with the Abraham story? Certainly not what I had been trained to do. Instead of using the reductionist models of the Enlightenment, I consciously adopted the new ways of reading the Bible that I had learned from Christians in the two-thirds world.[14] Instead of distancing myself from the text, pretending that the feelings and experience of people today were irrelevant, I actually began with them, and instead of working forwards from Bible times worked backwards from today's world, and then addressed questions to the Bible text in the light of contemporary life. Our typical approach has been to use the Bible as a window, through which we might gain some insight into the world of which it speaks. The only problem is that very few people can then make the leap back from that ancient world and apply what they learn to life in today's world. As a result, Bible study easily becomes a history lesson. It will be more helpful if we think of the Bible as a two-way mirror. We can see through it and back into its world. But we consciously allow the reality of our own world to be reflected in there, and use what we can see as a way of asking the Bible new – and relevant – questions. This way, we can expect to learn something about what God might be saying to us now, as well as what God said in ancient times to other people. 'We bring our experience *to* the Bible, we draw new insights *from* the Bible, we go back to our own situation *with* the Bible, and see it all in a new way.'[15] When you look at the Bible through the eyes of ordinary people, expect some surprises! And particularly when you open yourself to the kind of 'emotional exegesis' represented by mask-making, expect to be challenged yourself. But be assured that some exciting things are likely to happen when people realize that the Bible does after all relate to *the way they feel*, as well as to their mental processes. Incidentally, far from being a late twentieth-century idea, this was the way Jesus used his own Old Testament scriptures. Luke 24:13–35 (which we will return to in a later chapter) is one of the more striking examples.[16]

THE ENVIRONMENT

Not entirely unrelated to the way we use the Bible is the fact that many sensitive people are rejecting Christianity because they see it as having no relevant theology of the environment. An article written by Lynn White Jr back in 1967 has been quoted so often, it hardly seems necessary to repeat it here. But it is worth reflecting on what he wrote, for it is an opinion widely shared today not only by card-carrying activists in the environmental movement, but by many others:

Christianity in absolute contrast to ancient paganism and Asia's religions ... not only established a dualism of man [sic] and nature but also insisted that it is God's will that man exploit nature ... Christianity bears a huge burden of guilt ... We shall continue to have a worsening ecological crisis until we reject the Christian axiom that nature has no reason for existence except to serve man.[17]

Scientists continue to debate the precise extent of the environmental crisis we face. But no one can deny that there is a crisis, whatever its proportions. After all, if the hole in the ozone over Antarctica is as big as Europe, then the world has to be in poorer health than if there was no hole at all. And most people believe that, if there is a solution somewhere, it will definitely have no connection with Christianity. One of the major claims regularly made in support of New Age spirituality is that, unlike Christianity, it is environmentally friendly, because it regards the whole cosmic system – people included – as joined together in a deep spiritual unity. Many Christians dismiss environmental concern as irrelevant to the task of evangelization, and regard people like Lynn White as ill-informed and irresponsible. There is certainly a lot of misinformation being put about concerning Christian attitudes to the environment, and it does no harm to point out that Christians have not spoiled things single-handedly. The Baltic Sea is at least as polluted as the Mediterranean – and that was the work of an atheistic communist ideology, while Buddhists in Thailand started cutting down rain forests there at least fifty years before anyone in the Christian west thought of doing the same thing. But that is the easy part, for it is absolutely undeniable that the leaders of the Industrial Revolution who start-

ed all the pollution were Christians, motivated not only by the
Calvinist work ethic but also by the conviction that God had
put the world and its resources at their disposal. They were of
course also deeply influenced by the secular materialist values of the Enlightenment, with its pretentious optimism about
human potential – but this self-centred individualism in turn
nourished its roots in the insistence of Reformed faith that
every individual is solely responsible *for themselves* to God,
with an inevitable corresponding reduction in responsibility
both towards other people and for the wider environment.

This is one of those points where Christians need to be prepared to live with their past, and accept responsibility for it.
Repentance might be a more appropriate attitude than self-
justification. But we also need to do some hard thinking about
our own theology, especially notions of the fall, sin and blessing.[18] Three assumptions about the environment seem to per-
meate the thinking of many Christians. First, that creation
exists solely for the benefit of people, and therefore can be
exploited no matter what the cost. Second, that God is entirely
transcendent and 'out there', totally separated from creation
and no longer involved in it. And third, that everything physical is sinful in comparison to the spirit or the powers of reason. Put otherwise, many Christians have a Newtonian view of
the universe in which everything is a big machine operating
according to fixed 'laws of nature'. Therefore, while Christians
might believe God created the universe, many also believe
that God lost interest in it because of sin – and that is why
people have to manipulate it as best they can for their own
benefit.[19] This understanding has prevailed for the greater part
of the last 200 years, if not with the explicit approval of
Christianity, then certainly with no effective opposition from

it. I remember hearing an American tele-evangelist taking part in a debate on Christian attitudes to the environment, and he put it bluntly: 'animals belong to the jungle,' he said, 'and men [sic] belong to God.' He might have been a chauvinist, but he was certainly not out of tune with the Christian tradition. Back in the 15th century, Thomas à Kempis said much the same thing, albeit in a less strident way: 'Every time I go into creation, I withdraw from God.'[20]

Historically, many Christians have been uncomfortable not only with the physical universe, but with their own physical existence, which is one reason the Church finds it so incredibly difficult to make any useful contribution to current debates about the nature of sexuality. Christians who think of the fall as a hierarchical tumble from spiritual perfection to material sinfulness are bound to regard the physical as second-rate and spiritually unsatisfactory. This view itself owes a lot to our self-centred western individualism, and beyond that has its philosophical roots in the ancient Greek dualism between matter and spirit. The Bible, however, takes a broader view of both fallenness and redemption, in which sin and salvation are not about metaphysics but about relationships. A spirituality that regards the created world and our own physical existence solely as a backdrop for personal salvation has an inadequate understanding of sin, and consequently a deviant view of salvation.

Ex-Dominican Matthew Fox is right when he claims that too many western Christians are covert Docetists, more comfortable in the esoteric world of spirit than in the physical world God created – and his concept of 'original blessing' as the starting point for the Gospel has blown through much theological debate like a breath of fresh air.[21] Instead of a 'fall-redemption' model of Christian theology, he proposes a 'creation-centred spirituality'. He argues that Christians should understand nature itself as a blessing from God, to be accepted and received – and by accepting ourselves and our own creativity, we will not only renew our own lives, but we can also enhance God's ongoing creativity by participating in that work. Fox traces an alternative Christian history exemplifying this paradigm shift, finding expression in the works of mystics such as Meister Eckhart, St Francis, St John of the Cross, Mother Julian of Norwich, and others. Temperamentally, I find myself attracted to much of what he says, though Fox's analysis is undoubtedly too simplistic. In particular, he is inaccurate in his historical analysis, and all those he mentions as having a 'creation-centred spirituality' also had an awareness of sin as an objective moral reality. Fox is unrealistically optimistic about human nature, and as a result he is unrealistic about sin, especially the experience of the marginalized and oppressed who find themselves systematically sinned-against.[22] Having said that, however, we surely need to be reminded that fallenness is not something that exists or happens without people. The essence of sin is a breakdown of relationships – between people, between people and the natural world, and between people and God. This understanding is basic to any talk of effective evangelization, for our view of the nature of sin and blessing (and the relationship between them) affects our understanding not just of the environmental crisis, but issues of gender, race, economics and other aspects of our broken world to which Christ offers wholeness.

PEOPLE AND THEIR NEEDS

In the light of these considerations, our understanding of people and their needs should also be re-examined as Christians face the responsibility of discharging a renewed evangelistic calling. Just as the world has changed rapidly, so people's needs have changed enormously. At the time of the Reformation, the prevailing problem was how to deal with personal guilt. Martin Luther himself was a striking example of that. A century ago, in the time of the great Victorian evangelists, many people were terrified by death and what might follow it in 'eternity' – and as a result, that theme featured prominently in many of the hymns written at that time. Today, the great need of people all over the world is to find personal fulfilment and a sense of meaning in life. A recent study of the faith journeys of new converts in England showed that a massive 49 per cent of them came to faith in Christ without any sense of guilt at all – and only 18 per cent felt some specific sense of guilt related to their own personal shortcomings.[23] At the same time, virtually all of them defined the Christian life in relationship terms – with God, with other people, and with themselves – rather than in terms of specific beliefs in theological or doctrinal propositions.[24]

At a time when there is such an obvious identity crisis in the wider culture, it is only natural that the same search for new definitions and directions should also dominate the personal agenda of individuals. We see this not only in the lives of those who are unchurched: it is also a central concern of many Christians as well. Unfortunately, while people are engaged in the spiritual search at the level of personal meaning, the Church as an organization often finds itself locked into the concerns of the past, and perpetuating the language, structures, forms of worship and personal expectations that served our predecessors well a hundred or more years ago. How else can we explain the enormous dissatisfaction about the Church that seems to exist even among those who are committed to it? We need to be proud of our past, while recognizing that what suited people then is unlikely to be appropriate today. Of course, no church is literally the same today as it was a century ago – not even those that pride themselves in not having changed! But what a tragedy if we eventually manage to pull ourselves into the 20th century just as the rest of the world moves into the 21st.

People today are searching for meaning predominantly in terms of renewed relationships, and this need for someone to love and someone to be loved by begins in the home. It has been shown that integration of the family is a key factor in the life of growing churches: 'many churches which have children participating in the adult services, ... which emphasize the importance of reaching out to family units, have grown. With the family unit under threat today, opportunities to participate in an activity with all the family can appeal. Many families want to give their children a religious upbringing. Involvement of the family lessens formality but part of the spirit of the age is the spirit of informality.'[25] The same finding has something relevant to say about strategies for evangelization: 'many churches have found that reaching families as a unit can be more successful in winning men than concentrating on men alone.'[26]

Under the influence of Enlightenment values, have Christians become so aggressively individualistic that some of the most fundamental aspects not only of human life but also of the Gospel itself are being ignored? People interact with other people, and that is the context in which they find their deepest meaning and value. Jesus consistently spoke about the renewal of relationships as the heart of the Gospel, and when Paul reflects on the true meaning of salvation, he writes about the renewal of the physical environment, of human culture, as well as of individual lives, as all are transformed through the cross/resurrection of Jesus and the gift of the Holy Spirit (Romans 8:18–24). Taking all this seriously might well challenge not only church styles, but much popular theology as well.

A few years ago, I was involved in helping a woman at a time of crisis in her home life. She was on the fringes of Christian faith, and attended church from time to time though she probably would not have described herself as a believer. One day she came to see me. 'I've been reading the Bible,' she said, 'especially the bits about Jesus.' She explained that, like many, she was attracted by what she read, and could easily follow Jesus. 'But', she went on, 'I really have enough problems of my own without joining the church.' That phrase has stuck with me ever since. In a world that is fragmented at so many levels, people are searching for acceptance with no strings attached. How can we affirm broken people and lift them up – and then challenge them to discipleship? Jesus had a unique capacity for doing both those things, while we find it so difficult to do either.

THE NATURE OF GOD

When Christians talk of sharing their faith, who is the God whom they are trying to communicate? For many people today, this question focuses on the kind of imagery used to describe God. Traditionally, God has been described in exclusively male terms, even by those who would argue that God is without gender, and recognize that the Bible itself has any number of passages where female imagery is applied to God (eg Deuteronomy 32:18; Isaiah 42:14, 46:3–4, 66:12–13; Matthew 23:37). Some Christians – especially in Britain – are inclined to dismiss debates on such matters as trendy nonsense. But it is a serious issue and we neglect it at our peril. The truth is that it is about far more than just language. In Marshall McLuhan's well-known phrase, 'the medium is the message'.[27] The language we use both influences and articulates our whole understanding of who God is and the ways God works. To give a very simple example, in a world of abused families the imagery of mothering is likely to be far more user-friendly than the language of fathering. But it goes deeper than that. Is God angry or nice? What does God require of people? What kind of response are we looking for when we share the Gospel with those who as yet are not Christians?

When Jesus was asked that kind of question, he gave a very interesting answer. Quoting from the Old Testament book of Deuteronomy (6:4–5), he repeated something that his questioner no doubt already knew: 'You shall love the Lord your God with all your heart, and with all your soul, and with all your mind, and with all your strength ... and you shall love your neighbour as yourself' (Mark 12:29–31). Western Christianity has typically majored on just one aspect of that exhortation. We tell ourselves that following Jesus begins in the mind. Our thoughts are important, and getting our thinking organized theologically so that we believe the right things is of the essence of Christian conversion. But according to Jesus, the way we think is only 25 per cent of the total picture. People are more than just minds. How can we engage other parts of ourselves in the process of spiritual discovery? Ministering to the cognitive part of someone's personality is easy to do. Restricting one's own faith to thinking is relatively unthreatening, which is probably why so many of us do it so enthusiastically. It also has a history in the sort of Christian thought that owes its inspiration to Greek philosophy, encapsulated at one end of the historical trajectory in the words of Philo of Alexandria ('We must keep down our feelings just as we keep down the lower classes')[28], and at the other in the aphorism of Descartes: 'I am thinking, therefore I am.'[29]

Jesus, however, calls disciples to something different. Ministering to the emotions ('heart'), or the body ('strength'), not to mention that intangible spiritual core ('soul') is more complex and demanding, which is probably why most churches never really engage with people at those levels. George Bernard Shaw once said, 'Few people think more than two or three times a year. I have made an international reputation by thinking once or twice a week.' Have our churches become attractive for just one sort of person (the bookish), and is that why we find it more and more difficult to communicate in an increasingly visual and tactile age? It was Charles Darwin who first noticed the significance of non-verbal aspects of communication, and it is a topic that is highly relevant to Christian evangelism.[30] According to Albert Mehrabian, words account for only about 7 per cent of the total impact of a message, while 38 per cent of it comes from vocal messages (tone of voice and so on), and a massive 55 per cent is non-verbal – or body language.[31] Other studies rate the influence of the non-verbal even more highly.[32] A traditional Chinese proverb expresses the same thing more simply: 'I hear, I forget; I see, I remember; I do, I understand.'

Expressing all this more theologically, most of us in the west have felt happy to concentrate almost exclusively on understanding God as transcendent and all-powerful. Like many other aspects of our history, we cannot change this, though we should not be surprised by it. At a time when our culture was driven by imperialist expansion into distant lands, it was convenient for our forebears to have an imperialistic God. In Europe, most church buildings reflect power and authority, not only in their actual construction but also in the way people congregate in them. To sit in rows is to model a transcendent view of who God is.

Two things in particular make me uneasy with all this, one of them theological and the other more practical. In theological terms, few would disagree with the statement that the incarnation is the heart of the Gospel. But the incarnation is not about transcendence and power. Quite the reverse. If almighty God had wished it, God could no doubt have entered our world as a full-grown, macho adult male. Notwithstanding the imagery of some traditional hymns which convey that impression, that is not how it was (not according to the New Testament anyway). At the centre of the Gospel is the fact that God became a child. Weakness, vulnerability and powerlessness are central to Christian belief – and to the extent that Christians fail to model that in both lifestyle and evangelistic communication, they are betraying the very Gospel that they claim to represent.

This theological observation relates also to a practical issue. For in a generation which has rejected the trappings of transcendence and imperialistic power (and that means the majority of today's spiritual searchers), we will not make much progress with a purely transcendent Gospel. I would go so far as to say that our perpetuation of overt images of transcendence is actually impeding the evangelistic task. If we truly believed in a God who is 'in the midst', many things would have to change, among them our buildings, styles of worship, and the ways we teach and expect people to learn.

PRIORITIES FOR THE CHURCH

It is no surprise, then, to learn that we shall need to re-examine our priorities as churches. Much of the present concern is with our own organizations. Many churches are simply so hard to join that not many will make the effort. This particularly affects churches which would describe themselves as 'gathered congregations', where there are often so many hurdles to be jumped and hoops to be gone through that it is a wonder anyone at all ever makes it through to full acceptance and membership. Those inside tell themselves these things are necessary in order to preserve the purity of the church. To those outside, they look suspiciously like barriers specifically designed to exclude everyone else. 'Most people are not attracted to active, closed groups, which can often function like pressure groups. If Christianity is to increase it will be by people joining us not because they have to, but because they want to. We must show love not just for one another but for those outside too. Bridges must be built into the non-Christian world.'[33] To take this seriously is likely to be a more painful process than many people imagine.

I have a Christian friend who works with drug addicts in Edinburgh, and I remember her telling a story about one particular addict who was in the final stages of breaking free from his addiction. In order to help him through this time, my friend had committed herself to being with him as near to twenty-four hours a day as she could possibly manage. It was demanding, but if he made it she knew it would have been worth the effort. One day, he said, 'There's a big horse race on today, and I need to place a bet.' Now my friend was one of those abstemious Christians who had never in her entire life contemplated the possibility even of going into a betting shop, let alone placing a bet on a horse. As a matter of fact, she was unsure whether or not she approved of such activities. You can imagine her moral dilemma when this person made such an announcement. Did she let him go by himself – and maybe risk him dodging off somewhere else to purchase drugs? Or did she put her scruples to one side, and go with him? She decided on the latter course of action. There was just one outstanding problem: she had never been inside a betting shop before. She began to wonder what people do in such establishments. Do they stand up, or sit down? Do they talk to one another? And so on. She began to appreciate that it would be extremely threatening to go through the door without having at least some idea what might meet her on the other side. Then she came up with a brilliant plan. The betting shop was on the opposite side of a rather busy main road, with a pedestrian crossing almost directly outside the door of the shop. They would walk to that crossing, and while waiting for the traffic to

stop she would take a good look through the window and see
what everyone else was doing. That way she would be prepared for the experience. Her plan worked like clockwork –
until she lifted her eyes to look across the road into the window. Anyone who has ever tried to look into a British betting
shop will know why. The windows are all blanked out by law,
precisely to prevent people outside from seeing what goes on
inside! 'I was terrified,' she subsequently reported, 'as we
walked through the door my heart was beating so fast I thought
I would pass out. It was one of the most horrific experiences of
my entire life.' And that was from someone working regularly
with drug addicts!

As I heard that story, I made some immediate connections
with the Church's evangelistic task. Have you ever tried to
look through the windows of a church? Crossing the threshold
of a church building is likely to be a highly threatening experience for most people in today's world. 'What is it like
inside?' 'What do people do?' 'How can I be sure I'll not do
the wrong thing and embarrass both myself and the rest of
them in there?' These are just some of the thoughts that will
no doubt cross the minds of those few who even entertain the
possibility of a visit to church – while the rest (the majority)
will just find the whole idea so threatening (not to say irrelevant) that there is no way they would ever venture onto such
alien territory.

Most modern evangelism is on our territory, in places and
circumstances where Christians feel safe because they know
the ropes – and where others feel threatened because they
don't. We will not reach many people that way. On the other
hand, there are many signs that in places where *we* might feel
threatened, God is at work in people's lives. If we take seri-

ously the example of Jesus and the practical implications of our incarnational theology, then we are the ones who will need to allow ourselves to be threatened by sharing the good news on territory that to us seems foreign. There is no shortage of evidence that people today are engaged in a desperate search for new spiritual meaning in life that will transform them as individuals and in relationship with other people and with the planet. But where are the Christians who will get alongside them in such a way as to facilitate the search?

There is a group of native Americans who used a simple signal on the doors of their homes to indicate whether or not they were ready to entertain visitors. The door was secured by a catch on the inside, which when lifted opened the door. In the middle of the door was a small hole, through which a rope could be passed to connect with the catch on the other side. Any visitors seeing the rope knew they were welcome. Without further ceremony, they simply pulled on the rope, the catch was raised, and they went in. If there was no rope showing, the message was simple: the inhabitants were not able to receive visitors. All over the world today, the ropes are hanging out of the doors of people's lives in a very obvious fashion. They are ready to receive visitors who will facilitate their spiritual search. Even twenty years ago, they were not so likely to have an open door. No one knows for how long the present spiritual search will continue, though it is a safe guess that it will last at least into the opening years of the next millennium. But how can Christians grasp the rope and enter as welcome guests, so that their message will be recognized for the good news they believe it to be? That question must now occupy our attention for much of the rest of this book.

chapter three | Back to the Beginning

Effective evangelism requires an understanding of our cultural context, sensitivity to the needs of people, awareness of the radical demands of the Gospel, and willingness to commit ourselves to it. So what more obvious thing to do than to go back to our roots in the New Testament and the life of the early Church for inspiration? Surely, if any Christians ever knew the secrets of successful evangelization, it must have been the apostles and their associates. No matter how familiar we might be with the New Testament stories, they still have the power to inspire and challenge contemporary readers.

It is easy to be excited by the heroic exploits of those first disciples of Jesus Christ, and modern Christians often wistfully imagine that if only they could get back to what was happening then, the Church's present problems would disappear. The massive expansion of the earliest Christian communities is certainly a remarkable story. Beginning with an untrained rabbi from Nazareth, assisted by a collection of hill-billies from rural Galilee, it is the kind of rags-to-riches story that appeals to romantics and visionaries the world over. Though Galilee was probably not as unsophisticated as some modern commentators assume, the reality is that these people had very little going for them.[1] Their homeland was on the extremities of the Roman empire, and had it not been for its strategic position on the eastern frontier its inhabitants would undoubtedly have been dismissed as 'barbarians' by the sophisticated Romans and Greeks. As it was, they were always regarded as a cultural enigma: their long history, fierce nationalism, and unfamiliar religious attitudes were all but totally incomprehensible to Roman soldiers and politicians. Even within this maligned and misunderstood nation, Jesus and his disciples were out on the fringes. Galilee had an unenviable reputation, and in spite of being home to several leading rabbis it was frequently dismissed by the Jewish religious authorities as a place of no consequence. Moreover, most of the followers of Jesus were very ordinary people, with little educational background or personal career prospects. Without exception, they were the kind of people whom one would expect to make a minimal influence on their own culture, let alone change the whole world. Yet that is what they did, and within a generation of Jesus' death these same people had facilitated the establishment of Christian communities in every major centre of the Roman empire. Ultimately, of course, their mission was to change the whole direction of world civilization.

USING THE BIBLE

Faced with such extraordinary achievements, it is natural for modern Christians to look to the New Testament as the obvious starting point for all talk about evangelism. There are several good reasons for doing so. In terms of their practical performance, the earliest Christians – following Jesus' example and teaching – were singularly successful. Their strategy

worked, and there must be something that later generations of
Christians can learn from them. In addition, in terms of the
message itself, today's Church needs to have a sense of continuity with Jesus and the first disciples: how otherwise can
modern Christians be sure that what they are doing is
Christian evangelism?

But things are rarely quite so simple and straightforward,
and we also have to face some obvious challenging facts about
the Bible. We are not the only people to be inspired by the
stories of the New Testament. Nor are we the first. If Christian
witness was just a matter of reading and understanding what is
in its pages, and then acting on it, the world would presumably have been evangelized long before now. There is the further fact that the Bible by itself seems to be of limited value in
the evangelistic task. People do become Christians through
reading it, of course. I was one of them. But that is exception-
al. Bibles have been readily available throughout the western
world for the last hundred years or more. The UK has one of
the highest rates of Bible availability anywhere in the world –
yet its churches are in serious decline. It is not without reason
that the Bible has been dubbed 'the least-read bestseller', and
despite the multiplicity of modern translations now available
people still pronounce it difficult to understand. Even when
people get around to reading it, they understand the Bible in
different ways. The parable of the Good Samaritan and the
story of Abraham have already been mentioned. All the various ways of reading those (and other) stories are perfectly
valid. To make progress in communicating the Christian faith,
the Church needs to take seriously the possibility that there
may be no such thing as *the* message of the Bible, and that it
might quite legitimately mean different things to different peo-

ple. In any event, the starting point has to be people's current understandings – whether or not they happen to conform to the expectations of those already in the Church.

Different theological traditions will have their own ways of handling these particular challenges. But all need to appreciate that before we commit ourselves wholeheartedly to the search for New Testament ways of doing evangelism, we should think carefully about the most appropriate use to which we can put the Bible in Christian mission today. We can probably all agree that, to have integrity in their mission and message, the faith and practice of modern Christians must be continuous with that of Jesus and the earliest disciples. But that is not the same thing as merely trying to replicate their mission, and it certainly does not imply that we somehow need to take ourselves back into their world in order to be authentically 'Christian'. There are a few relevant considerations of methodology here. For example, not a single New Testament book was actually written for the purpose of providing its readers with models of evangelization. The book of Acts arguably comes close to this with the way it describes a variety of typical mission situations. Even here, though, it would be foolish not to recognize that there is an enormous cultural leap from life in the ancient Roman empire to the complexities of modern western culture. The mere fact that a particular methodology features in the New Testament does not mean we should – or could – apply it across the board in today's rather different world.[2]

Even when it is possible to identify insights that seem relevant to contemporary circumstances, it is important to preserve the integrity of the various New Testament authors, and not do violence to their original intentions. In every case, they organized their materials for other purposes than those for which we might now wish to use them. In particular, we cannot be sure that the Bible writers included all they would have wished to say on a particular subject, had they been given the space and opportunity to do so. Every New Testament book was provoked by specific circumstances, and to a greater or lesser degree those circumstances influenced the selection of subject matter and the way it is handled. In their enthusiasm, modern Christians often forget this, especially when dealing with the New Testament letters. Each of these is, in effect, only one half of the story. Reading a letter written by Paul, for example, is like eavesdropping on one side of a telephone conversation. We all know the challenges that presents! The amount of sense we can make of the overheard dialogue will depend on how well we know the person engaged in the call. If we know the people at both ends of the line, then we will have more chance of making sense out of the exchange than if we know only one of them. But even then we are unlikely to grasp what is being said with 100 per cent accuracy. If that happens when we try to understand half a conversation between people we know, and who live in the same world as we do, with similar cultural experience, then imagine the difficulties in spanning the centuries and trying to discern the nuances of what is now a non-existent half of a correspondence on theological issues between Paul and one of his churches![3]

Ordinary Bible readers are not the only ones who underestimate the difficulties. Professional theological scholars do the same, and their over-confident pronouncements on the nature of the circumstances addressed in some of the more complex New Testament books do nothing to encourage the sort of restraint that will serve us best in sharing faith with our contemporaries. Unfortunately, some of the New Testament books which look as if they could be most useful are also circumscribed by the most problems. Corinth, for example, is perhaps the nearest we come to a New Testament model for a church in something akin to a modern multicultural urban environment – yet it would be a bold person indeed who claimed to know with any precision exactly what was going on there at the time Paul was in correspondence with them. The same is true of the gospels. Like the New Testament letters, they too were theological documents written to address particular needs. Their portraits of Jesus present him as he was relevant to the concerns of their original recipients. This is not to say that the New Testament is of no use in today's evangelistic task. On the contrary, if we know how to ask the right questions it can have considerable value, which will be explored in some detail in later chapters. But we do need to acknowledge its limitations as well as its potential.

How then can we use the Bible? That depends what we want to use it for. In terms of evangelism, there are two ways of looking at it. First, how may we use this remarkable book as itself a tool for evangelism? And then, how can we use it as a guide to appropriate models of evangelism that will reflect the central values of the Gospel?

THE BROADER PICTURE

Effective evangelism is not the same thing as persuading people to read the Bible. But that does not mean the Bible is irrelevant or useless in faith-sharing. As a matter of fact, if it is important to preserve our own continuity with Jesus, then we cannot do without the Bible, because (in spite of all its limitations) that is the only place where we can have any sort of access to knowledge of the teaching of Jesus and the lifestyles of the earliest churches. The Bible is a vital ingredient in the mixture that is successful evangelism. But it is only one ingredient, and not the whole mixture. At least three elements are involved in communicating Christian faith to people in today's world, which we might describe as three different – though related – kinds of stories.

God's Story

First of all, both theologically and strategically, is God's story. Many Christians look out from the embattled cloisters of their church buildings and wring their hands in horror at what they see around them in today's world. 'Where is God?' they ask – and not a few conclude that God has somehow given up on our world, which is presumably why they then develop a faith that seems more concerned with the work of devils and demons than about God and the Holy Spirit. If that is our starting point, need we be surprised if evangelization never gets very far? It is a mistake to suppose that evangelization depends on Christians doing things for God. To imagine that God is somehow helpless, locked away in heaven with no capacity to do anything unless Christians set up evangelistic programmes, is to have a very impoverished – and maybe heretical – notion of who God truly is. The Bible emphasizes that this is God's world, and God is at work in it. Moreover, God sometimes works in the most unexpected ways. When the prophet Isaiah contemplated the plight of his people exiled in Babylon, he knew that God was at work in the great movements of world politics that would ultimately lead to their release and return to their homeland. Cyrus, the Persian emperor who overthrew the Babylonians and replaced their policy of transporting the peoples of occupied territories by a more humane approach, was so much in the centre of God's will that the prophet described him as God's 'messiah', the one anointed by the special grace of God's Spirit (Isaiah 45:1). Cyrus was not a Jew of course, nor did he ever become a convert, but because he upheld values and standards that were central to the biblical faith, Isaiah had no hesitation in declaring that God was working through his empire in a very specific way. It is not difficult to identify similar happenings in today's world, where many of the most remarkable changes of recent years obviously reflect the values of God's Kingdom – things like the demise of totalitarian communism, as well as the rise of the new spiritual search in the west. The message is clear: God works not only through self-confessed Christians, but in many other ways through people of goodwill who (often without knowing it) share Gospel values.

Those who accept the Bible's starting point – that people are made 'in God's image', and the whole creation is something of which God approves – will not be surprised by that (see Genesis 1:1–31 and the repeated refrain that God regards the world as 'good'). Jesus himself accepted this biblical faith in God as creator and sustainer of all things, and the way he used imagery from the world of nature conveys the clear message that God's activity can be discerned in it. Paul saw God at work not only in the world of nature (Colossians 1:15–20; Romans 8:19–23) but also in the world of other religions. On his arrival in Athens he was confronted with hundreds of altars to every deity imaginable. Nineteen centuries later, a

western missionary to Africa encountered similar scenes and
dismissed them with the observation that 'When I carry my
torch into the caves of Africa, I meet only filthy birds of darkness ...'.[4] Luke specifically records that Paul was 'deeply distressed to see that the city was full of idols' (Acts 17:16). But
it was not Paul's style to denigrate and belittle the beliefs of
others in this way, any more than it had been Jesus' approach
before him (Luke 9:49–50). Far from condemning it all, Paul
saw that God was at work even in this ostensibly hostile environment, and recognized an opportunity to share his own faith
by identifying his Lord with the 'unknown god' of Athenian
spirituality.

The Bible unhesitatingly affirms that God is constantly at
work in the world in many ways, times and places. Evangelism
is not about Christians working on God's behalf because God
is powerless without them. Effective evangelism must start
with recognizing where God is already at work, and getting
alongside God in what is going on there. God's story, not ours,
is the authentic starting point.

I learned this lesson personally in a striking way back in
the 1980s, when I was Mission Convener of the Scottish
Churches Council. In 1986, I was invited, along with the cap-
tains of Scottish industry and leaders from other walks of life,
to a promotional presentation by a company which had been
commissioned to organize a Garden Festival in the city of
Glasgow, as part of the urban renewal programme for British
cities that was in full swing at the time. The event was to be
held over a six-month period a couple of years later, and the
message was simple: 'If you have a product to promote in
1988, do it at the Glasgow Garden Festival.' It so happened
that we did have 'a product to promote': the Scottish churches

had just agreed to celebrate 1988 as 'Year of the Bible'. Not long after, my partner and I found ourselves sitting with the chief executive of the Garden Festival company, asking if at some point in the year a small corner could be made available for the churches to celebrate this particular project. The conversation inevitably turned to the Bible. 'Why do you think people would be interested in the Bible anyway?' was the question – in response to which we enthusiastically pointed out the historical importance of the Bible in our culture, and the significance of its message for today.

The executive evidently got the message – or decided to call our bluff! At any rate, he commented that if the Bible was as important as we were claiming, then we needed not just a small corner, but the whole place in which to celebrate it. As a result, we were offered the entire 120-acre site for one of the major Christian festivals: Pentecost Sunday. More than that, the company running the Garden Festival would finance the event! After all, they were paying entertainers on other days throughout the summer season, and to them Pentecost Sunday was just another day. There was a catch, of course: the Scottish Churches Council would have to come up with enough Christian artistes and performers with sufficiently varied skills to provide a balanced programme throughout the whole site for the whole day. That was quite a challenge, because it amounted to over a hundred programme hours. However, not only did it all come to pass, but with an attendance of over 47,000 it proved to be the largest single event to take place throughout the entire six months for which the Garden Festival was open – and in due course the organizers received a gold medal from a government agency to prove it! I learned a lot from that experience, not least that God is at work in the world – and probably moving well ahead of us – even before we do anything. The apparently unChristian world of western culture is nothing like as hostile to the Gospel as some Christians like to think. Why? Because this is God's world, and God is at work in it. 'Out of the mouths of infants ... and of secular business people' (Psalm 8:2; Matthew 21:16).

Bible Stories

Then there are the Bible stories – with their excitement and conviction, and of course, their discontinuities and apparent contradictions. Every Christian knows what might be called the main story-line of the Bible, which describes God's definitive actions in history. The creation, flood, promise to the people of Israel, the exodus, the Law, the prophets, Jesus Christ, the gift of the Spirit, and the life of the early Church – all these things are so central to the Bible's message that they have often been called 'salvation history'. But every Bible reader also knows that these are not the only things in the Bible. There is a lot of other stuff in there as well – and it is not all such good news. Alongside the Sermon on the Mount are any number of bloodthirsty Old Testament heroes, many of whose exploits are so horrific they would still be classed as criminals even in today's violent society. We would certainly find it hard to commend them as role models for serious searchers after spiritual truth. If we had a next-door neighbour who treated his wife and children the way Abraham did, we would all report him to the police – and our unchurched neighbours would do the same. The Bible has unquestionable strengths. It also has embarrassing weaknesses. It has the power to attract, and the ability to repel. Just as it is possible to play down the fact that God is at work in the world, and as a result end up with a feeble definition of evangelism that amounts to people doing a good turn for God, so it is possible to play down and ignore those parts of the Bible that might be said to be evangelistically counter-productive. To use the Bible meaningfully, we should take account of all that.

You might be forgiven for supposing that up to this point sharing faith sounds like sharing theology: ideas about how God works in the world, notions about the Bible and its contents, all presented in a more or less impersonal, almost intellectual kind of way. We have been rather good at doing this in western Christianity – but it has not led to effective communication of the Gospel. If a purely cerebral, rational faith could change people, the western churches would not be where they are today. Living in Scotland with a rich theological and intellectual heritage, I am particularly conscious of this. Historically, we have had so much theology, and so many Bible teaching sermons (almost 500 years' worth since the Reformation!) Yet theology and Bible reading and study seem to have made little effective difference to the moral and spiritual state of our nation. I have spent much of my life studying theology and preaching sermons, and I would not wish to deny the usefulness of either. But we have to face the facts, however unpalatable they may be for our favourite theories and ideas. The faith of the Church has an objective content that needs to be communicated. That refers to what Christians corporately and historically believe. But the faith of the Church is also the faith of *people*. In that sense it has a subjective element: it refers to what particular believers have found to be true in their own experience. For evangelism to be effective, we need more than just God's story and the Bible stories.

Personal Stories

So the third crucial element must be our own personal stories. The First Letter of Peter 3:15 puts it well with the exhortation that Christians should 'Be ready to give an account of the hope that is within you'. Effective evangelism happens, first, when Christians listen to other people's stories (their own experience, and the stories they recount as a way of making sense out of it all) – and then continues as we share with others our own stories, reflecting our experience of life, and enable them to appreciate what we have discovered about the meaning of it all. Jesus was an expert at this kind of communication. As the gospels depict him, his conversation typically had two main features: he asked questions, in order to elicit other people's stories – and in response, he told his own stories. When we preach sermons, or hand on ready-made summaries of Christian belief and theology, we inevitably present ourselves as experts. Doing it that way, it is all but impossible to avoid giving the impression that we are people who have it all together, people with no questions. But when we tell stories, we reveal ourselves as weak and vulnerable – spiritual pilgrims with whom others can identify. The truth is that we have something to share with others not because we are different from them, but precisely because we are no different. Yet we easily forget that, and 'evangelism' becomes little more than a sharing of theological and doctrinal propositions.

Think of these three things as three circles. At the point where the circles intersect, that is where effective evangelism takes place.

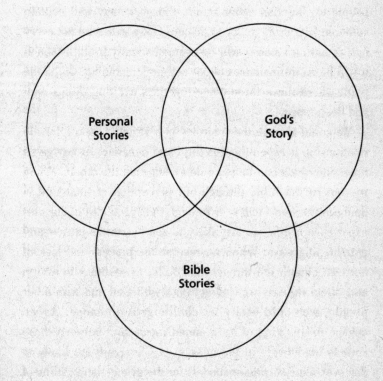

Notice, of course, that only a very small part of each circle intersects with any of the others. Not everything that God is doing in the world will of itself lead to people becoming disciples of Jesus Christ, though it may well extend the influence of God's kingdom. Not everything that is in the Bible will draw people to Christian commitment, though it may well contain valuable lessons as we try to discern God's will. And not every part of our own stories will be evangelistically fruitful, though it will be an intrinsic part of our self-understanding. But at the point where these three come together, exciting things can, and do, happen.

We could arrange these circles in a variety of ways, for the relationship between them is fluid and dynamic. At any given time, one circle can be more dominant than the others. When we look at the Bible through our perception of what God is doing in the world today, or through the spectacles of our own experience of life, we are likely to see its stories in new and enlightening ways. When we reverse the process and look at our own church life through the Bible, to enable it to inform and direct the way we interact both with God and with other people, we could easily be challenged to change. As we engage in this kind of open-ended interaction between these various ingredients in the mission of Christ, we are likely to discover some surprising models for the evangelistic calling of the Church today.

THE GREAT COMMISSION

The remainder of this chapter will explore some of the ramifications of all this in relation to one of the best-known evangelism texts of the whole New Testament. This is Matthew 28:16–20, the so-called 'Great Commission'. Its words are familiar: 'Go therefore and make disciples of all nations, baptizing them in the name of the Father and of the Son and of the Holy Spirit, and teaching them to obey everything that I have commanded you. And remember, I am with you always, to the end of the age.' Coming as it does at the end of Matthew's account of the life and teaching of Jesus, it occupies a strategic place in this gospel. Some commentators find it a surprising way to conclude a gospel that in other respects can seem very Jewish. Perhaps Matthew was not so narrow-minded as he has sometimes been imagined to be. In any event, this narrative is not everyone's favourite Bible passage. Over the centuries, it has been used and abused for all sorts of disreputable purposes. In the hands of medieval European kings, it stirred the passions that led to the Crusades. In the thinking of the Conquistadores, it justified the forcible 'conversion' to Christianity of the native population of South America. And in the hands of the modern missionary movement in the 18th and 19th centuries, it moved European explorers not only to great personal sacrifice, but also on occasion to an unbridled nationalistic fervour that has led, with some justice, to the criticism that missionary endeavour was often just one aspect of western imperialist ambitions.[5]

In the light of Christian history, it is not surprising that some people find this passage unhelpful in thinking about faith-sharing today. But it is strategically important in the New Testament. By placing it at the end of his gospel, Matthew effectively presents it as Jesus' last will and testament, his final instructions to the disciples who were to continue his message and ministry. Scholars have questioned whether

Jesus himself would have spoken these precise words, with their careful use of a Trinitarian formula. Whatever the answer to that question, it is obvious that the disciples believed Jesus had commissioned them to continue his work, and certainly by the time Matthew put pen to paper towards the end of the first century, this vision was so obviously coming to fruition that it could not be questioned that it was the Lord's will for his Church. Moreover, when we look at it closely and compare it with the style of Jesus' own life, not to mention the motivation and achievements of his immediate followers, there are very good reasons for supposing that the understanding of mission presented here accurately reflects Jesus' distinctive attitude.

One thing that stands out is the sheer breadth of the definition of evangelism in this passage, incorporating at least three main concerns. First the message is to be taken out, as the disciples are told, 'Go to all peoples everywhere'. Then is the importance of communication: 'make them my disciples'. Finally comes spiritual growth, for there is also included here the injunction to 'teach them to obey everything'. It is worth spending some time to look at these in turn.

Taking the Message Out

This raises a question of method. Just exactly how is the good news to be shared with other people? The New Testament provides several answers to that question, and the one given here needs to be balanced with the others. But this one is distinctive enough to be worth pondering. Notice where Jesus starts. 'Go into all the world', he says to the disciples. This is a startling emphasis for a religious teacher, who might perhaps have been expected to exhort other people to 'come in to the church'. Certainly within the Jewish context, Gentiles were always welcome to learn about Judaism by choosing to go into the synagogue, and becoming converts if they wished. But to go out and share the faith overtly with others would not have been part of the religious culture in which the disciples were raised. Quite apart from that, there were other reasons why going out must have been the very last thing the disciples were wanting to do at that point in time. There was a hostile world out there, which had little time for Jesus himself, and even less for them. By the time Matthew wrote his gospel, much of the Church was already suffering considerable persecution. But the seeds of it were there already in the weeks immediately following the first Easter. Jesus himself had been crucified, and the most obvious thing in the world would have been for his followers to lay low at least for a while. But Jesus was clear and categorical. If God's Church is to do God's will, then God's people need to be mobilized. They need to share their faith with other people wherever they are. The needs of the world, not the concerns of the Church, are primary to an understanding of effective evangelism. The rest of the New Testament shows that this conviction was clearly a major key to the success of the early Church. They went out, taking their message to where other people were. They met them in the streets (Acts 2:1–42), the market-places (Acts 18:1–3), the lecture halls (Acts 19:9–10), even on occasion in the sacred shrines of other religious traditions (Acts 3:11–26; 14:8–18).[6] When they worshipped they did not typically do it behind closed doors (Acts 2:46–47), and even the Eucharist was an opportunity for witness to unbelievers (1 Corinthians 11:26).

It is always easier – and certainly more comfortable – to meet other people on our territory than to venture to join them

on theirs. It is considerably less threatening, because that way
Christians can control what happens and ensure that no-one
says or does the 'wrong' thing at inconvenient times. But on
this point the message of the New Testament is unequivocal:
the Church is most true to its calling when its people are
mobilized to look beyond themselves and out into the world.
Evangelization is not about inviting the world to come into
church buildings and look at us, if they are interested. They
are generally not.

None of this is likely to be completely new to readers of
this book. Most people who have ever seriously contemplated
the evangelistic imperative will be familiar with the need for
the Church to 'go out'. But here is a further question prompted
by this text: how are we to go? The modern Church does not
typically go from a position of military strength. That, we tell
ourselves, is a regrettable feature of our past history that is
now mercifully over. But it is still all too easy to espouse a
cultural and personal imperialism which leads to a form of
mission that can become a mere processing of people so that
they become like us – and so particular styles of dress, language or speaking are promoted, as if being Christian was a
matter of being like we are. No doubt it is possible to understand this passage in an imperialistic way as saying, 'Go and
conquer the world with the Gospel'. But only by ignoring its
total context.

We read this New Testament story with the benefit of hind-
sight. We know as a matter of historical fact how this small,
dispirited and disorganized band of people had in the course
of less than a generation taken the message of Jesus not only
to their own people, but to every major town and city in most
of the known world of their day. To later Christians, they are

heroes. But who were they really? How would any of us have responded to this great commission if we had been there? I think I know the answer to that question for myself, and it would have been fairly negative. 'But surely, Lord,' I might have said, 'you can't be serious. Just let us enjoy our own experience of your presence – keep to ourselves the little bit of happiness and meaning we have. There's a hostile world out there, you know, and we've already had enough trouble without deliberately looking for more.' The text itself indicates that this is exactly how some of them did react. From the point of view of an evangelistic strategy, the most important statement in here is found not in the great commission *per se* but in one of the preceding verses: 'When they saw him, they worshipped him, even though some of them doubted' (Matthew 28:17). There is not much sign of imperialistic self-confidence here. This is not the militaristic clarion call of 'Onward Christian soldiers marching as to war'. On the contrary, Matthew depicts a group of people whose starting point is their own weakness – people with at least as much doubt as faith, who were prepared to go out onto other people's territory, not to conquer it but with an overwhelming sense of their own inadequacy and vulnerability.

Throughout their evangelistic ministry, two things characterized these early disciples: commitment to Christ, and weakness in the face of the world. They did not share their faith from a position of strength, seeking to boss people into the Church like some kind of spiritual sergeant-major. They shared from a position of being in solidarity alongside other people, recognizing that they too had their weaknesses and doubts. To go out in this way was truly an act of faith for Christ's followers – committing themselves to something unknown and personally threatening. Remember, 'the medium is the message' – which in evangelistic terms means that 'Churches are free to choose the ways they consider best to announce the Gospel to different people in different circumstances. But these options are never neutral. Every methodology illustrates or betrays the Gospel we announce. In all communications of the Gospel, power must be subordinate to love.'[7]

Communicating the Good News

This raises two questions: What is the message? and How are people persuaded by it? We will come back to the actual content of the Gospel later. Here we shall focus on its communication, though if the medium truly is the message (and that concept is not at all alien to the teaching of the New Testament), we can never entirely separate the two.

My daughter must have been about four at the time. The two of us were wandering around a park in one of our large cities. It was an autumn morning, with pale sunshine just beginning to penetrate the mist, and the smell of wood smoke was in the air. One minute we were laughing and chatting as we ran at top speed through piles of dead leaves, scattering ducks and geese as we went. The next, we were deadly silent, looking for squirrels in the bare branches of the trees around us. As so often happens on such occasions, fun led to serious reflection, and as yet another pile of leaves went flying in all directions my daughter asked, 'Daddy, do you think God is at the bottom of everything?' In the split second that it took me to decide exactly how to reply, our spiritual musing was interrupted by a commotion in the bush right next to where we were walking. Before I had time to realize what was going on, a middle-aged man dressed in a grey raincoat and clutching a tiny brown-backed book, jumped out directly in front of us and without further introduction fixed his piercing eyes on me. 'Tell me, young man,' he insistently demanded, 'are you saved?' I remember being relieved that he was not the kind of person who actually wanted an answer to his question. His main purpose was to detain us for long enough to give me a quick summary of Peter's sermon on the day of Pentecost, and then to read a few New Testament passages about how I was 'living under law' when by taking his advice I could actually be 'living under grace'. With a final quick exhortation to 'Think about these things before it's too late', he disappeared with a flourish into the bushes whence he had come – no doubt to materialize in some other part of the park where he would seek to evangelize other lost souls who were also wasting their time on trivialities such as discussing the meaning of life with their children. Certainly, I couldn't help contrasting the two conversations. And my daughter's response to this intrusion was interesting, if predictable: 'Daddy, what did that man want?' It was much harder to give a satisfactory answer to that question than to the first one she had asked!

We smile at that kind of story, but it is typical of so much that passes for evangelism in the modern western Church. Imagine now a church on Sunday morning, full of people. 'Hundreds are being reached', the church leaders tell themselves, as the earnest preacher at the front expounds the Bible. 'The teaching in our church is second to none', they boast, though in truth they are only expressing admiration for their minister's remarkable ability to speak for fifty minutes without a break – for not too many of those present are moved by what they hear, and probably the church has had no new members for quite some time. Take a closer look at their faces, and you can begin to understand why. Many of them are bored to death. They like to give the impression that they are listening eagerly to every word of it, and some of them even look as if they are writing it all down for future contemplation. Mark you, the preacher is not fooled quite so easily. Probably half of them are writing next week's shopping list, while those who seem most engrossed in the pages of their Bibles are reading something quite different than the passage being expounded – and a good half of the congregation are handing sweets round and trying to dispose of the wrappers without being seen. Many of them are wishing they were somewhere else. In desperation the preacher – who is a good and gifted person – concludes that these people, though they are in church, are closed to the Gospel. For their part, the congregation wish it was all on the TV, so they could switch it off and get on with something more useful. It sounds exaggerated? A 1989 survey of British churchgoers discovered that some 42 per cent of them admitted to falling asleep in church. More than a third looked at their watch in church every Sunday, and an amazing 10 per cent owned up to putting their watch to their ear and shaking it, because they thought it must have stopped. Though only 4 per cent always wished they had stayed in bed on a Sunday morning, 67 per cent admitted they often felt that way.[8]

What is happening? Probably there is a lot of talking, but no communicating. What the preacher and church leaders think is 'teaching' is not translating into learning. Yet no one has been taught until someone has learned something. Transmission of the message is just one small part of the total

process that leads to understanding. It is only the first stage –
and the easiest one. The others – communication and acceptance – are much more difficult to achieve. A great deal of
so-called Christian evangelism is really just transmission of
the message, but that is not the same thing as effective reception of it. There is an old definition of a lecture as 'a transfer
of material from the professor's notes to the students' notes
without it passing through the minds of either'. A lot of what
Christians label 'evangelism' is just like that. We seem to
imagine that people's heads are empty, and once we have
learned the knack of prising the lids off them we can pour in
the substance of the Gospel, and our responsibility to communicate the faith has been fulfilled. But people are not like that.
'Heads are neither open nor hollow. Heads have lids, screwed
on tightly, and no amount of pouring can force ideas inside.
Minds open only when their owners sense a need to open
them. Even then, ideas must still filter through layers of experience, habit, prejudice, fear and suspicion. If ideas make it
through at all, it's because feedback operates between speaker
and listener.'[9]

We all have filters. They are an indispensable part of who
we are, and contain everything that we know and believe: our
worldview (basic values and beliefs about life); our experience
and learning (those things we believe to be true); and our personality. We all use our filters all the time, to sort out information that comes our way. If we did not, we would soon be sub-
merged by it. Think of what happens in your home when there
is a commercial break on the TV. In a typical home, someone
might go to the bathroom, another to the kitchen, others may
engage in conversation. Very few will watch the commercials
unless they have a specific interest in the products being

offered. A lot of people react that way to anything connected with the Church. An earnest Christian couple knock on a door to evangelize the people who live behind it. A man answers, the callers announce they are from the local church – and what happens next? If the door is not closed immediately, there is a pretty good chance the man will call for the woman of the house. 'It's for you', he will say – because his filters tell him that, though he probably knows next to nothing about church, it is not something that relates to his life. The same thing happens elsewhere. It is currently trendy for healthcare professionals to minister to the 'spiritual needs' of their patients, but more often than not the church is perceived as totally irrelevant to this task – because most people filter out 'church' as being about joining an institution, whereas the spiritual search is something far more dynamic and relevant to ordinary people and the way they live. Our filters operate all the time, whether or not we are consciously aware of it. We can open them to varying degrees, depending on how we perceive the messages being presented to us. We can, and do, open them fully when we think the content of the communication is relevant for what we believe or need to have or know.

There are four elements in effective communication. There is the message (and the medium through which the message is channelled); there is the audience, and their responses; the process of feedback; and the communicator, with his or her aspirations and intentions. The relation between these four is cyclical, and there is no 'right' place to begin the process of communication, though Christians generally start with their message. They have something to say, therefore they search for the best words with which to say it. Inevitably, starting at this point they tend to choose words that suit themselves.

Christians are typically orientated towards ideas – either complex theological concepts, or something that looks much simpler but which in terms of communication still has inadequacies (an 'ABC of salvation'). The trouble is, most other people are somewhere else. Their starting point is not our message. I once heard a (slightly cynical) definition of a sermon as 'a set of answers to questions no one is asking'. I must have heard thousands of sermons that were like that: the only people who appreciate them are the ministers who preach them. Much of what we imagine is evangelism is just the same. Effective communication involves a lot more than merely presenting a message. This is nothing to do with the truth or otherwise of what our message is, for it is perfectly possible for a thing to be 100 per cent true, and yet totally irrelevant.

When my daughter was small, like many young children she used to get up very early each morning. This was no problem, except at weekends when the rest of us were not too keen to be roused at five or six o'clock! She soon got the message, and developed the habit of taking herself off to watch the TV, so that when I rose somewhat later I knew exactly where to find her and what she would be doing. At that time, there were very few programmes shown in the early morning on British television. More often than not she would be watching a programme connected with the Open University. The scenario was entirely predictable. 'What is this all about?' I would ask. And the reply? 'I don't know.' What she was watching was 100 per cent true – indeed, since it was usually some erudite professor exploring all conceivable angles on a subject, it sometimes seemed to me as if it could easily have been 150 per cent true! There was certainly nothing wrong with what was being said. Quite the reverse. And there would be people out there for whom it all made perfect sense. But so far as my daughter was concerned, it was totally and absolutely irrelevant to her entire lifestyle and understanding. Do you recognize the syndrome? Communication of the Christian message today is hampered not so much because we have an inadequate Gospel, but because so often it is simply an irrelevant Gospel. Those millions of people with a strong sense of serious spiritual search who appear to have no interest in the Gospel are not always rejecting the Christian faith. More often than not, they have no idea what it is. Christians think a message has been sent in their direction, but nothing has been received.[10]

To become the Gospel – 'good news' – the Christian message has to speak to the needs of ordinary people. There is nothing profound or new in that observation. The very first generation of Christians knew it well. Why else do you suppose they preserved four gospels instead of reducing it all to one comprehensive version of the life and teaching of Jesus? The answer is obvious. Each of the New Testament gospels was written as an evangelistic tool. Each is different, angled towards the needs of the various kinds of people for whom it was written. Moreover, the differences can in some instances be quite far-reaching. In the synoptic gospels of Matthew, Mark and Luke, the main subject of Jesus' teaching is presented as 'the kingdom of God'; in John, Jesus' teaching focuses on 'eternal life'. In the synoptics, Jesus' message is communicated through the use of story parables, in John the style is more elaborate (though still pictorial). Scholars have argued for centuries over which version more accurately represents Jesus as he really was. Maybe that is the wrong question, for surely this is an example of the flexibility with which the Gospel needs to be presented to different audiences, in order that it might become 'good news' in relation to their practical needs, concerns and interests.

To impose a uniformity on the Gospel, and force it into only one mould is to inhibit its effectiveness. In the first century, the adaptability of the Christian faith was its greatest strength, and the New Testament itself bears eloquent witness to how the situation and needs of those being addressed regularly determined the shape of the message. To stay the same, the Gospel must change. Even where human needs are the same, different languages and cultures require that the message speaks with different accents and tones. We can all see how the needs of today's people are different from those of the first century. Most of us can appreciate that the needs of people in the two-thirds world are different from those of the west. But needs differ not just from one culture to another. Even in one town, different communities will have different starting points. Spiritual and cultural discernment will be a fundamental part of successful evangelization. To be true to the New Testament, the Gospel needs to address these diverse needs with different emphases. This is one reason why evangelism is more than just transmission of theological or doctrinal propositions. It is not, of course, the only one, and in subsequent chapters we will explore others that are more specifically related to the content of the Gospel message itself.

Spiritual Growth

The third and final strand of the 'Great Commission' is what I have called the cultivation of spiritual growth and maturity. This is not the place to pursue this theme at length: it will

form the major topic of a subsequent chapter. But it is worth
noting here that Matthew includes continued growth in faith
as part and parcel of the task of evangelization. Jesus does not
send the disciples out to gain converts for a cause, or members for a church. He instructs them to make more disciples –
students, followers, learners, who are prepared to give all they
have in order to follow their leader. He does not look for people to 'make decisions', but to open their lives to the power of
the Spirit, so that they may continue to be challenged by the
good news. And by doing so, he clearly defines evangelism not
as an event, but as a process. Grasping hold of that will have
far-reaching implications for many areas of contemporary
church life.

chapter four | What is Conversion?

Two questions are never far from the centre of any discussion of evangelism: what is the Gospel, and what does it mean to be a follower of Jesus Christ? You might think that after centuries of theological debate and exploration, at least the answers to such basic matters would be settled and clear-cut. But these questions are not as simple as they sound. Ask any group of Christians to explain or describe their own experience of faith, and you can guarantee that there will be almost as many answers as there are people. But they will probably fall neatly into one of two categories, typically distinguished by their divergent understandings of the nature of conversion.

TRADITIONAL UNDERSTANDINGS

What exactly do we mean by conversion? For some people, the very word 'conversion' can mean only one thing: an abrupt crisis in life, in which everything suddenly and totally changes. To be converted is like stepping from darkness into light: before this decisive moment, a person is not a Christian, after it they are left in no doubt that they are. Over the centuries, there have been several outstanding examples of experiences of this kind. In his *Confessions*, Augustine describes how, as he sat in a garden reading Romans 13:13–14 in the late summer of AD 386, 'in an instant, as I came to the end of the sentence, it was as though the light of faith flooded into my heart and all the darkness of doubt was dispelled.'[1] More than a thousand years later, as Martin Luther sat in the tower of his monastery in Wittenburg, this time reading Romans 1:17 (supplemented by, amongst others, the writings of Augustine), he too had a similar life-changing experience. Two hundred years after that, on 24 May 1738, John Wesley's heart was 'strangely warmed' in London's Aldersgate Street, as he listened to a reading from Luther's commentary on Romans. These experiences were all different, of course. Augustine and Luther had both wrestled with the meaning of life and faith for a considerable time, while Wesley was already an Anglican clergyman, and indeed had led a mission to North America, before his 'conversion'. But that has not prevented many modern Christians (particularly those with an interest in evangelism) from identifying the single episodic crisis turn-around as of the essence of being and becoming a Christian. What is more, the model for such experiences is traced back to the pages of the New Testament itself. The story of how God dramatically laid hold of Paul as he approached the city of Damascus, intent on persecuting the infant Church, has been viewed as an experience to be savoured and actively sought after (Acts 9:1–9, 22:6–11, 26:12–18; Galatians 1:11–17). Evangelists who work on this model of conversion skilfully steer their hearers to a point where they are compelled to make radical decisions about their own lives, inviting them to follow Christ by going out to the front of a large crusade meeting, or kneeling at the penitent form of a local mission hall.

For many Christians, if 'conversion' means anything at all, then this is the only possible connotation it can have.

I remember visiting a large Presbyterian church in the USA. After the service, I was taken to the home of one of the pastoral staff, to meet his family and share their lunch. To have a visiting preacher from Scotland, the heartland of Presbyterianism, was obviously a very significant experience for them, and the whole family, well scrubbed and dressed in their best clothes for the occasion, were lined up in the hallway to meet me. I have no idea whether I lived up to their expectations, but I shall never forget what happened next. The pastor went from one to another, and then came to the youngest child, a girl called Lucy who must have been about seven years old. 'And this is Lucy', he said. As I greeted Lucy, I could hardly believe my ears as her dad continued, 'Of course, Lucy hasn't yet given her heart to the Lord Jesus – have you, Lucy? – but we're all praying for her. Who knows, maybe your visit will help her decide for Christ.' Well, how do you follow that in conversation with a seven-year-old? You might be forgiven for imagining that this child must have been some kind of uncontrollable monster who was virulently anti-church and unChristian – though in truth she was as well-behaved a youngster as I have ever come across. As we walked along the beach together later that day, Lucy revealed herself to be a girl who knew her Bible, who loved Jesus, and who was probably far more disciplined in her prayer life than I have ever been. I knew what was going on, of course, because this was not the first time I had met people like her father. So far as he was concerned she was a little pagan – and he knew that to be true because she had not yet adopted certain patterns of response to Christ which he was able to recognize and affirm as authentic. I did momentarily reflect that it was a strange family in which someone who was such an intense believer could manage to raise such a miserable sinner as he thought Lucy to be. I never asked that question, of course, for I knew what the answer would be: she had never come to a point of decision at which she 'gave her heart to the Lord', or got herself 'born again', and so by definition she was totally outside the grace and love of God.

During the same trip, I heard an evangelist speaking on American TV about New Agers who believed in reincarnation. 'I don't care how often you've been born,' he declared, 'if you've not been born again, then God has no time for you!' More recently, I was guest speaker at a week-long ecumenical Bible convention, and towards the end of the week I was cornered by an earnest woman who wanted to express appreciation for what I had been saying and doing. 'You're certainly different', she said – something with which I could not quarrel, and which I took to be a compliment. 'I can see you *really* love the Lord, and God is *really* using you ... but' [as she lowered her voice to a whisper, I sensed the punch-line was coming] 'are you *really* born again?' I knew what she was after, and I must confess that only served to ensure my response was more evasive than it might otherwise have been! Unless I could relate how I had come from a life of great sin to a life of fanatical faith in Christ, preferably as a result of some unbelievably striking, if not bizarre, crisis, then she found it hard to accept that I could possibly be, as she put it, a 'real Christian'. This is a very popular way of understanding the nature of the Gospel, and hence discipleship – and evangelism. I freely admit that, historically, it is Christians with this sort of outlook who have kept alive the evangelistic vision of the modern Church. For generations when mainline Christians were otherwise occupied, people seeking a 'born-again' experience were often the only ones calling the unchurched to faith. Moreover, I would be the first to accept that some people do have such dramatic experiences of God. But it is a serious mistake to universalize these into a model that everyone must follow, and to do so is likely to be highly damaging to the evangelistic enterprise.

BASIC QUESTIONS

The overwhelming majority of today's Christians do not have an understanding of God that is dominated by a dramatic crisis leading to major changes in their life. Many have grown up among other Christians, and never really found themselves rejecting faith in any profound way. Of course, they have had questions, and have frequently had to struggle to hold onto their trust in God. But they have never been against God in any fundamental way: as they have gone through life they have simply grown into a deeper understanding. Instead of experiencing a sudden U-turn, God seems to have kept these people in a straight line from childhood through to adult commitment, by means of Christian nurture in home and church. As a result, they find themselves embarrassed and confused when people call them 'unChristian' just because they are unable to identify a time when they were 'born again'. It is alien to their own experience, and as a result they are easily turned off by a concept of evangelism which for them seems to be focused in the wrong place. A major survey of British churches in the 1980s discovered that 'the actual word "evangelism" seems to be disliked by some as having a hard-sell connotation'.[2] Most Christians do not see faith as a commodity to be marketed, and while they would not deny the reality of dramatic experiences in the lives of those who have them, they would certainly wish to add that there is more to discipleship (and, consequently, evangelism) than that. If our holistic understanding of the 'Great Commission' is correct, they could claim to be following the example of Jesus in this.

It could be argued that the reason so many modern Christians have hesitations about this model of evangelism and conversion is because they have too little contact with those who are truly unchurched, and these are the people who are more likely to have crisis conversion experiences. There is no doubt that, if the Church is to grow, it will need to gain converts from outside. But there is no evidence that such people will typically meet God through crisis conversion experiences. *Finding Faith Today* is one of the most exhaustive studies ever conducted of the faith journeys of recent converts. Out of a broadly-based sample of 511 people who had made a 'public profession of faith' in the previous twelve months, 69 per cent described their coming to faith as 'gradual'. Moreover, even in churches describing themselves as 'evangelical', and therefore probably with a heritage that would tend to predispose them to assume the crisis model of conversion as the norm, only 37 per cent claimed to have had this kind of dramatic conversion, while the rest (63 per cent) described their faith journey as a gradual progression.[3] The report comments: 'The gradual process is the way in which the majority of people discover God and the average time taken is about four years: models of evangelism which can help people along the pathway are needed.'[4]

The simplistic view of conversion as a one-off, dramatic crisis experience must also be modified in the light of the teaching of the New Testament. Consider Paul himself. Whatever it was that happened on the Damascus road, it was part of his ongoing experience of God. It would be wrong to imagine that before this occasion Paul was a complete unbeliever. As a Pharisee, how could he have been? He certainly believed in God, lived within the parameters of a biblical morality, and expected the coming of the Messiah. These continued to be central pillars of his Christian faith, with the exception that he now identified Jesus of Nazareth as the Messiah. In terms of his own lifestyle, he was neither spiritually nor morally bankrupt at the point of his 'conversion'. Paul was not actively seeking deliverance from a threadbare Jewish spirituality that had proved unworkable, and the popular picture of a weary, guilt-ridden Paul trudging up the Damascus road full of doubts and self-pity, is a fiction. Many of Paul's most fervent admirers have popularized this image, not least Martin Luther, who experienced exactly that kind of release from his own guilt-ridden conscience. We need not question the reality of the spiritual experience of those who have such a life-changing escape from the bondage of personal guilt. But the mere fact that some of them found new direction through reading Paul does not mean Paul himself must have been like them. Reading Paul through the spectacles of his admirers is a dangerous business, and has frequently misrepresented both his personality (as dominated by guilt) and his theology (as dominated by sin and the concept of an angry God).[5] Paul never saw it that way. Looking back to his pre-conversion past, he described himself not as a guilt-ridden and defeated wretch, but as a self-confident, spiritually satisfied enthusiast

(Philippians 3:4–6). He was as sure as anyone could be that he was right, and that he was doing the will of God. The real challenge of the Damascus road was that he discovered he was wrong – and that is why his conversion affected every part of his being, and his theology had a place not just for personal needs, but had a social dimension, not to mention cosmic and ecological implications.[6] Conversion in the New Testament is not the spiritual equivalent of a trip to the religious supermarket in search of a new experience. It is far richer – and more challenging – than that.[7]

What then is conversion? Wherever we look in the New Testament, one thing seems clear: *change* is always very near the centre of the Gospel. No one ever meets Jesus and stays the same! At the beginning of his gospel, Mark summed it up in the familiar slogan, 'Repent and believe in the good news' (Mark 1:15). This was the message of Jesus in a nutshell, and it contains two elements: doing (repent) and thinking (believe). There is an emotive, intuitive element, combined with a rational or reflective element. Faith links together an objective and a subjective component. Both are important, though not the same.[8] This model of faith, with these two elements held together, should undergird all our modern methodologies for evangelism. It reflects the fact that deeds and words – actions and thoughts – were at the centre of Jesus' own evangelizing strategy. Disciples are committed to both – and bearing witness to both will make more disciples, and advance the Kingdom. It is worth emphasizing this, because a lack of balance on this point has been the cause of some of the most tragic – and unnecessary – divisions of twentieth-century church life. I refer, of course, to the division between the 'doers' and the 'believers', the social activists and the 'preachers of the Gospel', the so-called liberals and the card-carrying evangelicals. The social activists need to remember that without the proclamation of a message about Jesus, then there is little difference between Christian do-gooders and their secular counterparts. And the proclaimers need to remember that doing good is neither an optional extra, nor something that should be used as a carrot to attract people to the 'real thing' (preaching). It *is* the real thing.[9] At least, it was for Jesus, who spent a good deal more time doing than speaking, and in whose ministry the deeds generally preceded any words (which, when they were used at all, were often in response to questions that people asked about what he did).

This dynamic interplay between doing and thinking, repenting and believing, also functions as a model for discipleship. What was Jesus actually demanding of people? What did he mean when he asked for 'repentance'? What did he expect people to do? Certainly, a good deal more than marching to the front of a crowded crusade meeting and praying a prayer of commitment. More, even, than reading their Bible and praying and being a faithful member of their local church. Many studies of this Greek word 'repentance' (*metanoia*) describe it in terms of someone travelling along a road, and suddenly realizing they are heading in the wrong direction. As a result, they need to do a U-turn. We might also think of it in terms of someone climbing a mountain with friends, and becoming aware that others have found a better track, as a consequence of which they are making faster and more satisfactory progress. Such climbers know where they want to be, but are unsure of precisely how to get there. It needs someone on the higher track to show them the way and invite them to join it. In terms of the spiritual journey, that is what Jesus' call

to repentance is all about: changing direction, but to a place
that in your heart of hearts you knew you always wanted to be
anyway. Naturally, doing this means that a person's whole
lifestyle and values undergo a considerable change, so as to
reflect the claims of God's Kingdom. There is no shortage of
New Testament examples of the demand for such radical and
far-reaching discipleship, nor of those who were prepared to
accept it, as well as of those who were unwilling to pay the
price. 'Repentance' in this sense is a holistic notion. It affects
everything a person is and does. No area of human behaviour
is excluded.

Jesus also called people to 'believe'. Alongside demands
for changed behaviour and lifestyles, the gospels contain a lot
of theology, mostly open-ended theology designed to get people to ask questions rather than to present them with safe,
ready-made answers. Think of the way the key terms of the
gospels are open to so many understandings — phrases like
'the Kingdom of God', or 'the Son of Man'. Even now, scholars
are still debating the precise nuances of such teachings within
the context of first-century Palestine. Maybe we shall never
exhaust their significance, because Jesus actually intended it
all to be somewhat indeterminate. Parables are used in the
same way: there is never only one 'authorized' understanding
of what they mean. Jesus was intent on creating a space in
which people would be free to reflect on the significance of his
message for their own lives. Once a space has been created,
then the rest is up to God. The early Church was able to hold
together a vast and diverse spectrum of opinion, ranging from
those conservative Pharisees who were part of the church in
Jerusalem, to the liberal Paul and his mystical converts in
Corinth. But whatever the specific outcome, once a person has

met Jesus, the way they see things and understand and interpret them is radically challenged and changed. Belief is important, but it is not the whole of the Gospel. Theology and doctrine is central, but getting it sorted out is not necessarily the first step in the journey of faith.

PETER'S CONVERSION AS A BIBLICAL MODEL

If we now focus on a particular New Testament example, we may begin to see how all this works in practice – and what difference it should make to the evangelistic calling of the Church today. Next to Jesus, Peter is one of the most accessible characters in the gospel stories.[10] We know more about him than any other disciple, and his story obviously fascinated those early Christians who preserved it orally, and finally wrote it down. Here, we have space only to skim through some key aspects of his story. But as we do so, bear in mind that, as well as the relationship between doing and thinking, discipleship always seems to involve challenge and change, and ask at which points Peter was most truly and profoundly challenged to change. I believe that Peter's conversion to Christ is one of the foremost models of faith in the whole New Testament, and one that is of crucial importance today – especially for western Christians who find themselves needing to share the Gospel with successful people who apparently can manage their lives without God.

We can trace six stages in the discipleship of Peter, each one leading on naturally from the other.

1 Early Life
'I believe in God'

Peter was brought up as a Jew, so there was probably never a time in his life when God did not feature. He always believed something, and long before he encountered Jesus he would have some kind of faith understanding that had developed from his childhood. When Jesus had particular lessons he wanted the disciples to learn, he later chose children as their teachers – something that surprised the adults, but enabled Jesus to affirm his belief that children reared within a believing context were not pagans, and had a faith to share, however simply it may be expressed at that stage of their life (Mark 9:33–37, 10:13–16).[11] That was the starting point for Peter's journey into discipleship.

2 Call to Discipleship (Mark 1:14–20)
'Jesus seems a good guy'

I hesitate to call this story Peter's 'conversion', though on a common understanding of the term that is undoubtedly what it was. Before this encounter on the shore of Lake Galilee, he was not a follower of Jesus – after it, he was. Could there be a more profound about-turn than that? By any standards, whatever it was that happened to Peter and his brother Andrew on that day, was remarkable and life-changing. So what actually did take place? At first sight, it might look a bit like a classic crisis encounter. It certainly happened at a time in Peter's life when decisions tend to be made in those terms. For he was probably no more than a teenager – maybe even an adolescent, and at that point in life where we typically characterize and articulate things in terms of decision-making that will affect the whole future course of our existence.

Because of the crucial importance of this story, it will be worthwhile pausing to notice in more detail some of the things that were involved here. First of all, Peter was called to change direction: 'Come and follow me', said Jesus. In his mind's eye, Peter no doubt had a picture of what it meant to be successful. His life seemed to be running in well-defined directions. His father and grandfather had done it all before him, and he was building for his future on the social and economic successes of previous generations. He knew where he'd come from, and where he expected to go to. Yet Jesus says, 'Leave all that, you come with me!' 'You? Who are you?' Peter might reasonably have asked. There is more than a good chance that at the time Jesus was unemployed. As a local builder in the town of Nazareth, his business will almost certainly have had its share of the many lucrative contracts that were awarded in connection with the rebuilding of the nearby city of Sepphoris, but the project was completed not long before Jesus began his public ministry. It is tempting to think that he, and thousands of others, would be thrown out of work at that time.[12] Whether or not that is so, Peter must certainly have contrasted his own secure lifestyle with that of Jesus, who apparently had no regular home, and no prospects. Everything he knew about Jesus told him that he was not being offered fulfilment in life in the terms he had seen it before. He was not being called to join with the rich and powerful, but with the poor and the marginalized. It would mean a radical upheaval of all his social norms. Yet here was Jesus with this grand vision of God's Kingdom, and Peter recognized he was being presented with something that was big enough and good enough for it to be worth giving his life for it. 'As his disciples, we announce his solidarity with all the downtrodden and marginalized ... those who announce Jesus as the servant King ... are invited to enter with him daily in identification and participation with the poor of the earth.'[13]

Jesus also challenged Peter to change his priorities. Mark comments that 'at once they left their nets and went with him' (Mark 1:18). Can you imagine all the things they might have done first? But following Jesus meant that he must come first. To follow him meant things that had previously been of great importance now took a different place. Security, prosperity and a comfortable lifestyle were no longer of all-consuming importance. This must have been one of the more liberating aspects of being a disciple. Instead of being caught up in a life continually under pressure, Peter was offered a different direction. Leaving the nets was not a negative move, taking the easy way out by hiding from the harsh realities of life. It meant taking a new, positive – and challenging – direction in life and faith. The basic call of the Gospel is to follow Jesus!

Further, Jesus invited Peter to reassess the purpose of his life. 'What are you here for?', Jesus asked – to which the reply was, 'Catching fish – the same as everybody else.' The difference that Jesus makes is encapsulated in his call to 'Follow me and I will teach you to fish for people' (Mark 1:17). This takes us to the core of the challenge to discipleship. Peter needed to learn that discipleship is not a once-for-all thing, but an ongoing process. 'I will teach you', Jesus offered. But learning something about another person is not purely a cerebral affair. Obviously, facts and information are involved, but that is not the whole story – and in personal terms it is unlikely to be the first priority. When two people fall in love, their feelings are far more important than factual information about their partner. Things like a person's height, age, hair or eye colour, are not high on the list of things that one needs to know in a relationship. There, 'knowledge' is an altogether more personal thing, as you experience this other person, share yourself with them, and discover things that probably can't easily be put into words anyway. Western Christianity has too easily specialized in knowledge of theological and dogmatic propositions about Jesus, without creating space for disciples to 'know' him more closely. Peter made that mistake – and sometimes his grasp of the facts ran ahead of his personal knowledge. For him, the development of spiritual intimacy was ultimately to be one of the most threatening aspects of discipleship. Notice, though, that Jesus' purpose is not to teach disciples purely so that they can know a lot. What they have learned of him (and, no doubt, themselves) they are to share with others. These people were already good at catching fish: now they are to trawl for people.

So, we might say, Peter became Christianized. He became a disciple of Jesus Christ. His direction, his priorities and his purpose were all challenged – and he responded. He was converted. But was he? Certainly not by some modern definitions. From a twentieth-century perspective, what is missing from this story is at least as significant as what is included. We look to this story in vain for evidence of personal guilt, confession of sin, prayers of commitment, forgiveness, acceptance of theological dogmas, admission to the life of the Church, and all the other signs of commitment that have so often been identified as an indispensable part of 'the conversion experience'. Jesus demanded none of these, which would no doubt make him a very poor evangelist in the eyes of many today, for after all Peter only responded to the invitation Jesus gave him.[14] Of course, no one would seriously go along with that – would they? It seems that, according to Jesus, conversion is a much more complex business than many of his modern followers have allowed it to be – and it begins with the simple invitation to 'Follow me'. As we move on to subsequent episodes in the life of Peter, and unpack some of the other elements that were involved in his faith commitment, we will find ourselves forced to grapple with the possibility that by focusing on one single crisis experience, modern evangelism has trivialized the Gospel. Could it be that we fail to reach successful and satisfied people not because our message is too hard, but because it is not demanding enough?

3 Conversion of the Mind (Mark 8:27–30)
'I need to think this out'

Like the others who accepted Jesus' call, Peter spent much time in the presence of Jesus, watching what he did, hearing what he said, and discovering some new things about himself. As Peter got to know Jesus better, other challenges began to emerge, which he needed to integrate with his life experience and which demanded some response. Initially, Peter had committed himself to Jesus in the impulsive way that young people often do when confronted by charismatic figures. A young fisherman from rural Galilee instinctively recognized that Jesus was somebody new and different, apparently enjoying a more immediate relationship to God than many of the other rabbis who were around at the time – and certainly more open to sharing it with ordinary people. Peter knew he would have an instant rapport with this person, and so he was attracted. But as he got to know Jesus better, he began to understand that he was more than just a trendy radical. For one thing, Jesus' trendiness was obviously somewhat different from that of most wandering charismatic teachers of the time. His message was not really related to the political aspirations of his people, suffering as they were under Roman domination. Nor was Jesus very forthright in describing his own mission. The enigmatic term 'Son of Man' was his favourite title for himself, but no one had a very clear idea what that was supposed to mean – though its very mystique only served to emphasize Jesus' distinctiveness. As a result, Peter was forced to think. Who could this Jesus really be? As he reflected on that question, he began to reach new conclusions that broke the mould of his previous thought-patterns in a very big way. Mark highlights this by placing the conversion of Peter's mind at Caesarea Philippi. It was home to a shrine dedicated to the Greek god Pan, and also boasted a great marble temple built in honour of the emperor Augustus. An appropriate place, therefore, for Peter to reflect on the significance of Jesus in relation to other competing religious traditions. When challenged by Jesus' question, 'Who do people say that I am?', Peter's answer was unequivocal: 'You are the Messiah' – and in Matthew's version of the story, he adds, 'the Son of the Living God' (Matthew 16:13–20; Mark 8:29). For a Jew, there could hardly have been two more explosive concepts than these! His entire theology was blown apart – and remade.

The same thing frequently happens among young adults today, when as students they begin to think things through for themselves, questioning and clarifying the values of their parents. Peter never went to university, but he did leave home; and he spent time learning from Jesus. It was a time for talking things through, thinking new thoughts – and (as often hap-

pens at this stage of life and faith) crystallizing them into
hard-and-fast faith formulations, which sometimes manifests
itself in an abrasive attitude towards others. New understandings seem clear beyond doubt, though appreciating all their
implications may take much longer. This comes out quite
clearly in the experience of Peter, who in theological and
intellectual terms maybe got the words right, but had no idea
what they meant in terms of his own emotions or personal
commitments. In fact, when Jesus went on to explain what the
words really meant, Peter found himself unable to handle it.
His will was in tune with Jesus, and he knew he really wanted
to follow him: that was the lesson of Mark 1:16–20. His mind
was in tune with Jesus, and he was able to acknowledge him
for who he truly was: that was the lesson of Mark 8:27–30. But
his emotions were somewhere else altogether, and at this time
of clear intellectual challenge and change, he also found himself given a severe rebuke by Jesus (Mark 8:33). He was still
struggling to discover how to accept himself with his imperfections, yet be free to express his love for Christ.

4 Feelings in Crisis (John 18:15–27, 21:1–23) 'Can I really love him this much?'

Peter continues to play a major part in all the gospel traditions, living uneasily with the tension between motivational
and intellectual commitment, yet somehow unable to handle
his own feelings. This tension is only resolved towards the end
of the gospel story, in an episode that was so significant for his
spiritual journey that it features in all four Gospels. Peter's
uncertain emotional commitment to Jesus eventually surfaced
in the unexpected circumstances of the high priest's garden

after Jesus had been arrested, and was about to face trial for his life. This was a different situation from many of those Peter had previously faced. Here, merely using the right form of words to describe his belief in Jesus was not going to be enough. It was not so much that his theology was wrong or inadequate – just that theological formulations can never be the whole picture. In Peter's case, he was caught off guard by a simple question asked in a courtyard by an insignificant servant. If she had asked, 'Do you think this man might be the messiah?', Peter would have known the answer to that question, for he had sorted it out long before. Instead, she was more direct and personal, but for that very reason her question was a lot more threatening: 'You are one of this man's friends, aren't you?' (Matthew 26:69–75; Mark 14:66–72; Luke 22:54–62; John 18:15–27). Peter was not yet ready to handle a question couched in personal terms like that. A theological question would undoubtedly have been a lot easier. But this was different, for it impinged on Peter's internal spiritual search, and touched chords deep down in his psyche. It brought to the surface all sorts of uncertainties and hesitations that he had not yet felt able to handle. It revealed that though his basic life orientation – and his thinking – had undergone the sort of fundamental change we might call conversion, there were other areas of his personality that still remained fundamentally untouched by the Gospel: his emotions. This is a stage of faith which many modern Christians – especially westerners – find particularly threatening. A lot of people are much happier with rational, cerebral, theological beliefs than they are with something that will touch their emotions. As a result, they never face up to this kind of challenge, but are content to sit on the spiritual sidelines. Instead of following through the painful process of allowing the deepest recesses of their person to be challenged and changed by the Gospel, they prefer to stick with a cerebral, 'left-brained' understanding of faith. Perhaps this is where many so-called 'nominal' Christians find themselves. It is certainly where many men in particular are content to be.

How did Peter break through this tough challenge? We might debate which is the most appropriate New Testament passage to use to answer that question. In the context of Luke's gospel, it could well be the experience of the Day of Pentecost (Acts 2:1–42). In the fourth gospel, which I have chosen to follow here, it is a post-resurrection appearance of Jesus to Peter (John 21:1–23). Either way, it is only resolved as Peter allowed himself to be radically changed from the inside out. And the resolution of the problem was no less painful than his initial discomfort at realizing what he had done when he denied that he knew Jesus. In the story in John 21 Jesus invites Peter to make emotional commitments that, up to this point, he had been either unable or unwilling to make. Notice that Jesus did not cover the old ground again. His message this time was not, 'Come and follow me': Peter had already demonstrated his willingness to do that. Nor was it a test for theological soundness to discover if he still believed all the right things: Peter could have handled those questions. Instead, Jesus posed a question that Peter was much less comfortable with: 'Do you love me?' He tried desperately to avoid answering it, because it was challenging a whole area of his being that needed to be changed. But as he was able to respond to this renewed call to conversion, he found personal healing and fresh courage that moved him in a new and exciting direction. In due course in the experience of the earliest church, Peter's wholehearted commitment of his emotions to Christ was matched by the presence of the Spirit, and the next time he was challenged he was ready to go to prison (Acts 3:1–4:4). He had finally made it in his faith pilgrimage! Or had he?

5 Worldview Conversion (Acts 10:1–48)
'Who is God, who am I, what is it all about?'

How much of a person needs to change in order to be a follower of Jesus? All Christians recognize the essentially personal elements of morality and relationships that are included in conversion. But what about the Gospel and the public world? What about the big issues, the way we see the world? These are crucial questions for today – and the answer that Christians give will radically affect the progress and credibility of the Church well into the next century. How does the good news relate to our culture? It is not a coincidence that this question came to Peter as soon as he got involved with the business of evangelization. By taking seriously the call to share the Christian message with others, he found his most deeply cherished preconceptions about human existence were taken apart – and restructured.

Like all of us, Peter was part of a very specific culture. In his case, he made sense of things by thinking of the world in terms of relations between Jews and non-Jews (Gentiles). He was so confident that this reflected the ultimate truth of how things actually are that, though he was willing to share the message of Jesus with Gentiles, he felt it would only work if they could all be made into Jews first. Other people in his day thought in similar ways, though the terminology was different.

Educated Romans, for example, made sense out of the world by thinking of themselves as a cut above the unsophisticated and brutish 'barbarians' who lived on the fringes of the empire, while their entire economic and social system was based on maintaining the distinctions between slaves and free people, women and men, and so on.

Peter was challenged on this one when he received a call from the home of Cornelius, a Roman centurion (Acts 10:1–48). He immediately found himself in a turmoil, and it was a painful business to extricate himself from it. To him, everything about Cornelius was wrong: he was the wrong race, in the wrong sort of job, asking the wrong sort of questions. He couldn't possibly be the sort of person for whom the Gospel was intended. Now what was Peter's problem? It is easy to describe him as naïve, bigoted, or just plain stupid. But the real nub of the matter was that he had not fully worked out what it meant to be a Christian. Back by the shores of Galilee, he had been prepared to turn around and follow Jesus. Subsequently, his thinking and his emotions had been challenged. In fact, his entire lifestyle had changed at so many points that it felt as if he had literally given up all he had to follow Jesus. But there was one bit of his life that was a 'no-go' area for the Gospel. 'You cannot change the way things are', said Peter – and so the whole framework of cultural, political, economic and racial assumptions on which he had based his life was still unchallenged by his faith in Christ and, therefore, fundamentally unconverted.

He found himself learning some painful and difficult lessons. He was forced to admit that many of the things he thought were just 'the way the world is', were not that at all: they were a time-bound, cultural view of things. He also had to learn that the Christian Gospel must challenge the cultural assumptions on which people live. Disciples cannot keep Jesus shut up in one little compartment of life. It may be possible to be a part-time Baptist or Anglican (or Catholic, Presbyterian, Methodist, Pentecostal, or whatever) – but being part of God's Kingdom is a commitment that enfolds the whole of life. Evangelization is not just about private religious experience: it is concerned with the proclamation of a message that claims to be the absolute truth in all areas of life. For Peter at least, this was the most fundamental conversion of all. This time, his entire worldview was being challenged. His personal commitment to Jesus was in no doubt – but he still operated on cultural and political assumptions that at bottom were, so far, untouched by his faith in Christ. The story ostensibly tells of Cornelius's conversion. But if you ask who was the one who in this episode underwent the most traumatic challenge to change, then it certainly was not Cornelius! 'The call to conversion should begin with the repentance of those who do the calling, who issue the invitation.'[15] The relevance of all this to the evangelization of today's world hardly needs to be highlighted.

6 'Sharing myself and my faith'

The rest of Peter's story is less accessible to us because of the nature of our sources in the New Testament. No doubt like many modern Christians, his faith development did not proceed unhindered in a straight line from simple beginnings to maturity. There would be times when he went back and questioned his intellectual commitment to Christ. There would be other occasions when he was forced to work through again and again the depth of his emotional conversion. And we know for certain that he found it hard to accept the challenge to his worldview that was involved in following Christ. Long after the Cornelius incident, he was in conflict with Paul over the same questions (Galatians 2:11–14), and as late as the mid-fifties he was still sufficiently narrow in his outlook for some legalists in Corinth to claim him as their patron (1 Corinthians 1:12, though they may have been using his name without his permission or encouragement). Following Christ is often like that, as we move in and out of different stages of faith at different points in life. Think of it as like a long coiled spring, in which progress from one end to the other often feels like going round in circles, but nevertheless there is still a progression forwards from one end to the other.

Certainly, in Peter's case there was no doubt about his fundamental hopes and aspirations. He joined with enthusiasm in the evangelistic calling of the Church, first in Galilee, then in Antioch, then travelling through much of the empire before arriving in Rome, where his commitment met the ultimate challenge, and he did not flinch from giving his life for the Christ he loved so much. Through much turmoil, many blind alleys and not a few mistakes, Peter still turns out to be a powerful role model for all subsequent generations. Or, more exactly, it is precisely because of the turmoil, the blind alleys and the mistakes that his willingness to give all he had for Christ seems so encouraging to others. For is not this the stuff out of which discipleship is made, and in the midst of which the concept of conversion takes a form that is anchored in the everyday experience of real people?

SIGNPOSTS FOR FAITH-SHARING

Finally, let us come back to our starting point. What was going on here? If you like, at what point did Peter become a 'real' Christian? When was he truly converted? Three comments might help to give direction to such enquiries.

Firstly, we should note that in the course of the years of his life to which we have access in the New Testament, Peter was growing up. Probably he was little more than a teenager when he first met Jesus, and the narratives all indicate ways in which he was growing: physically, spiritually, morally and personally. Growth in all these areas was running parallel. People respond to God in different ways at different stages of growth. Not just in terms of physical growth, as we mature from childhood, through adolescence, to adulthood – but in personal growth continuing through the whole of life. We are all persons in the process of becoming somebody, and sensitivity to where people are at in their personal maturity will be an integral part of responsible evangelization. 'The response of faith is to present as much as one knows of oneself to as much as one knows of God.'[16] There is an appropriate response to God for different stages of life. When my daughter was about eighteen months old, I remember her looking me in the eyes and saying, 'I love you, Daddy' – and then adding, 'I love Jesus too'. That was an appropriate response to God for a child of that age. Of course, she expresses her faith differently now, and no doubt when she is as old as I am she will have different responses again. To insist on processing people so they all look like peas in a pod is not the Gospel. People do not have experiences – they are experiences. Wherever we look in the Gospels, awareness of this was always Jesus' starting point. That alone is a good enough reason for us to take it seriously.

Secondly, crisis points played a key role in Peter's experience. I remember my friend Raymond Fung (former Evangelism Secretary to the World Council of Churches) drawing my attention to the Chinese character for 'crisis'. It is actually two characters, which together mean 'a dangerous opportunity'. People are at their most vulnerable during a crisis, yet at that time they are also most open to change: 'the impetus for movement is frequently an event or experience in our lives over which we have little control ... a health crisis, change in relationships, models of others we want to emulate, a teacher, reaching personal limits, deep questions about oneself, being hurt, responding to others' needs, experiencing God in a new way, telling your own story to another, loss of a relationship, death, developing a quiet time, losing truths once held dear, longing for God ... at that moment in our journey we have a choice. We can choose to plunge ahead not being afraid of change, or we can turn back by blocking our feelings and not dealing with the issue. This can be a critical time.'[17] If the Church is to fulfil its evangelistic calling, then it needs people who are sensitively aware of the crisis points, both in their own lives and in the experience of others.

Thirdly, notice how often other people played a key role in Peter's decisions to change. Crisis points by themselves do sometimes lead to faith experiences, and there seems to be a significant number of people who without any contact with a church or Christians find themselves drawn to Christ at such times.[18] But more often, it is other people who are instrumental in facilitating the spiritual quest. Jesus himself played a key role in Peter's faith story, gently challenging, and setting up signposts to send him off in new directions. This is a skill we must explore further in a later chapter. But sometimes, it was other people who were not necessarily disciples themselves. The servant in the high priest's garden, and the searching Cornelius, both played a significant part in Peter's personal journey of faith.

This chapter has deliberately focused on a particular New Testament example of conversion in all its multifaceted diversity. But the same conclusions could be reached by different routes. In reflecting on the experience of Peter, I have frequently been impressed with the way in which it parallels many of the findings of Christian educators who have explored the meaning of faith from the perspective of developmental psychology. I am thinking in particular of the work of James Fowler. Taking his cue from Erik Erikson's identification of eight distinct stages in human development, from cradle to grave, Fowler pinpointed what he called six 'stages of faith'. The precise nature of these stages is open to a good deal of debate, and Fowler and others have refined the model many times since the idea was first put forward.[19] One version to which I find myself particularly attracted (maybe because it reflects my own spiritual journey fairly accurately) is that proposed by Janet Hagberg and Robert Guelich in their book *The Critical Journey*. This is not the place in which to engage in an extensive comparison of these various understandings of the nature of faith and conversion, but it is striking how easy it is to place the New Testament model of Peter alongside these others, and appendix 1 indicates how this might be done.

In terms of practical evangelization, the most striking conclusion is that the New Testament, the experience of the majority of Christian people, and contemporary developmental thinking all converge in suggesting that conversion to Christ is not a single event, it is a process. But there are many events in the process, and all of them present significant opportunities for the sensitive evangelist to nurture spiritual growth and challenge to new levels of commitment. No one can doubt that our culture is engulfed in a growing search for meaning. If we can understand the nature of the spiritual search going on among unchurched people today, it might also give us some clues as to how the successful person who says, 'I have no need for God' can be reached with the good news about Jesus.

chapter five | Evangelism and Worship

It is not fashionable to put together the two topics with which we are concerned in this chapter. Writing back in 1965 Donald McGavran, the founding father of the church growth movement, drew a strong distinction between worship and evangelism. 'Worship is good,' he wrote, 'but worship is worship. It is not evangelism.'[1] McGavran subsequently modified this strident statement a little, but the notion is still widely accepted in one form or another. In *The Logic of Evangelism*, Professor William Abraham also makes a strong distinction between evangelism and worship.[2] And at parish level, as the church of the 1990s searches for an instant formula for evangelistic success, much attention is focusing on the concept of so-called 'seeker-friendly' services. Here too a good deal of emphasis is placed on the notion that, to be 'seeker-friendly' to today's spiritual pilgrims, worship must be given a low profile, if not locked firmly in the closet. Many are now claiming that worship is something that suits Christians, but alienates those who are not yet committed. As a result of this philosophy, thousands of churches are experimenting with a form of evangelism which specifically excludes the experience of worship as being, at best, irrelevant to the whole business of calling women and men to faith in Jesus Christ, and, at worst, as an alienating experience that might actually prevent people from following Christ.

These ideas, and others like them, are undoubtedly trendy. But they should not be accepted without close scrutiny. Paul wrote of the importance in his own ministry of being prepared to 'become all things to all people, that I might by all means save some' (1 Corinthians 9:22), and that is a sentiment with which I find myself in complete agreement. There are many places in church life where we need to be more adventurous, and faith-sharing is certainly one of them. In particular, I would say we need to be more creative in exploring how faith can be shared not in church buildings (where Christians feel comfortable), but in the spaces and places where other people feel safe (and Christians may feel more vulnerable). At the same time, however, Christian evangelization is not concerned with marketing and packaging a commodity that is to be bought and sold in the supermarket of faiths. The spiritual journey – conversion – is about people being caught up into the presence of God, and responding in ways that will move them on towards that total commitment to Christ which, according to the New Testament, is at the heart of discipleship. Worship plays a key role in that kind of faith journey. Other types of experience (in particular, left-brained, cerebral experiences) may well point people in that direction, but they are not an end in themselves. Effective evangelism and renewed worship are inextricably linked. You cannot have one without the other, and to try and do so will lead to serious imbalance. Churches that are unprepared to face up to the challenge of renewal in worship will easily turn evangelism into just another marketing exercise. Churches that focus exclusively on their own internal spirituality will easily become introverted and irrelevant to the needs of the world. But put the two together, and you have an exceedingly powerful, and faith-enhancing, combination. Keeping them apart may be easier – and it certainly reflects the reductionist approach of traditional western thinking. The widespread dissatisfaction in our culture with this way of understanding things is in itself a good enough reason for asking if the separation of evangelism from worship does not owe more to cultural conformity than to spiritual integrity. But there are also more substantial reasons for taking another look at this topic.

It is undeniable that worship and evangelism are inextricably linked together in the New Testament. Wherever we look, worship is absolutely central to the life of the early Church. Dynamic worship was a major factor in the rapid growth of the earliest Christian community from an insignificant group of Galilean peasants to become a movement that shook the Roman empire to its foundations. When John's gospel depicts Jesus speaking of how God's glory in the Church would be recognized by those outside, and attract them to the Gospel (John 17:1–26), it was not just wishful thinking, but a reflection of what had actually happened in the Church by the time the fourth gospel was written. Moreover, wherever the Church is growing today, worship is at the centre. In world terms, those western churches that appear to be growing without a renewal of worship are the exceptions that prove the rule.[3] On a global scale, more people are attracted to discipleship by worship than by any other single factor, including most of the things to which we conventionally attach the label 'evangelism'. Moreover, worship has led to remarkable church growth in many countries where any kind of overt Christian evangelizing activity is forbidden. China is a classic example, where

for decades the Church has grown underground as Christians
have worshipped, and as their non-Christian friends have
been drawn into a context where there was a sense of the presence of God.⁴ But it happens in other places too. A Roman
Catholic bishop whom I know was visiting an Islamic country,
where Christian evangelism was officially forbidden. The only
thing the Church could do was worship – and they did. At the
end of a Eucharistic celebration, a group of Muslim men made
their way to the front of the church. Not knowing what was
going to happen next, my friend assumed the worst, and
thought their presence could only mean one thing: trouble. In
fact, they said they had been so impressed by the unspoken
message they had received merely by watching what went on,
and appreciating for the first time the true meaning of the
bread and the wine, and the good news that lay behind it all,
that they wanted to know more about the Christian faith. They
were not drawn to Christ by an evangelistic sermon, still less
by an apologetic lecture – for they had heard neither. All that
happened was that they sensed the presence of God in the
worship, and knew it was for them.

That kind of thing happens all the time all over the world.
Why does it take us by surprise, when the New Testament
itself describes the Eucharist as 'proclamation', that is, witness? In 1 Corinthians 11:26, Paul uses an unusual Greek
word (*katangello*) when he says that in the Eucharist 'You *proclaim* the Lord's death ...'. Elsewhere in the New Testament
the same word is used of proclaiming the Gospel (Philippians
1:18, Colossians 1:28). The significance of the experience of
authentic worship for faith has always been tacitly recognized
in our credal statements. The old Scots Catechism asks, 'Why
was I created?', and responds with, 'I was created in order to

worship God ...'. Much modern psychology has reached the same conclusion, namely that a sense of mystery, discovered and expressed through something like worship, is basic to the human condition. This is a constant thread that runs through much of the thinking of Carl Jung, for instance, and explains the popularity of mystical experiences among spiritual searchers in the western world today.[5]

There is also an obvious theological reason for linking worship and evangelism. We have already noticed how Matthew's 'Great Commission' identifies spiritual growth as part of the evangelistic task of the Church, while our discussion of conversion pointed in the same direction. If discipleship is a holistic call, encompassing the whole of life, then evangelization needs to have the same quality. If scripture, theology, history, and the experience of the world Church today all seem to bring evangelism and worship together, then we need very strong and compelling reasons for separating them, even (or especially) if we do it as some kind of marketing device to make the Gospel 'seeker-friendly'.

WHAT IS WORSHIP?

One of the few books written in recent years which seems to me to have any kind of prophetic insight into the nature of evangelism is *The Isaiah Vision*, by Raymond Fung. He identifies three elements that are central: partnership with the world for peace and justice, the invitation to worship, and the invitation to discipleship. If he is right – and I believe he is – it will clearly do us no harm to take a fresh look at the interplay between worship and evangelization. Maybe we are asking the question the wrong way round. Could it be that some western Churches have a problem with understanding how worship can be evangelism, because they have a basic problem with their worship? 'To some Christians, the idea of inviting our ... partners and friends to worship with us is highly problematic. It could be embarrassing. The worship services in many of our churches are often either so uninspiring and clannish, or so unintelligent and unintelligible – or both – that we'd rather not invite others. If that is the case, we have a real problem on our hands ... How can we have the kind of worship to which we are not embarrassed to bring our partners and friends? Indeed, how can we have the kind of worship that may expose others to an experience of God?'[6]

At a time when there seems little consensus on what worship actually is, or on what worship is supposed to accomplish, we need to start with some basic questions. What exactly do we mean by 'worship'? By way of exploring that question, come on a quick trip around three churches. Like me, you have probably visited them before, and doubtless noticed some of the same things as I have. The descriptions that follow are caricatures, of course. They are deliberately exaggerated (though not much), in order to highlight some distinctive trends. But, like all good cartoons, they are only overstating what is already there in real life.

Even to someone who has never been inside a church building before, the first one would probably feel vaguely familiar territory. In essence, it is an auditorium, not too different from a theatre or cinema. Certainly, everything happens up at the front, where the key players operate as if taking part in some kind of theatrical performance. I remember once leading a training course for people whose job was to welcome visitors to their church services. Part of the group exercises we engaged in was to identify the different types of people who might arrive at the church door, and to think about their likely impressions. One wit described the scene as he imagined an anthropologist doing research into human behaviour would perceive it: 'People standing up, kneeling down, closing their eyes, singing, going to sleep, paying money, eating sweets, and throttling children.' He was deliberately being cynical, of course, but he gave an accurate enough account of the behaviour that was labelled 'worship' in that particular church. In this sort of worship, the only person who really matters is the minister. If there was nobody there to carry through this role, then 'worship' could not happen: it would have to be called off. In recent years, some churches have modified this pattern slightly by trying to move away from the idea of a spiritual prima donna 'conducting a service' on behalf of the others, but they then typically replace the solo performance with a kind of variety show, in which other people move on and off stage basically to go through the same routines as the minister would have done single-handed in other circumstances.

This model of 'worship' is most likely to be encountered, on the one hand, in highly sacramentalist churches, and on the other (at the opposite end of the theological spectrum) in highly evangelical congregations. This pattern of worship conveys some interesting messages. To put it somewhat simplistically, if we adopt a theatrical model for worship, in which everything is in the hands of experts of one sort or another, merely acting as performers to an audience, then people will respond accordingly. They will see church as a show, and assume that once they have paid for it they have no further responsibility. They are quite likely to pick up the message that, whatever 'worship' truly is, it is something that happens exclusively between individuals and God. For many attenders at such services, the clergy almost embody God, and the whole language of the building and the service gives the impression that worship is oriented in only one dimension, namely the vertical. There is nothing horizontal, no sense that interaction with other people might play a significant part in it all. If people in this church inadvertently make physical contact with others (or do so at the 'wrong' points in the liturgy), they will back off very quickly and apologize as if they had committed an unmentionable sin. Which, in a way, they have, for they are not there to have dealings with other people, only with God. And even that is likely to be a one-way communication, as they spend most of the time sitting passively and listening to whatever is said from pulpit or altar.

Church number two is quite different. Almost the exact opposite, you might say. Many things will be tolerated here under the guise of 'worship'. To the casual visitor the whole thing might seem to be out of control, and certainly almost anything could take place. There is just one thing that seems consistent and characterizes everything else, and that is the necessity for the worshippers to lift their hands in the air in order to make anything happen at all. This is the sort of church where you can easily imagine a vote being taken by people putting their hands down instead of up. I remember visiting a church like this in California, which had an amazing building, including a whole series of fans on the ceiling to help keep the congregation cool during the hottest part of the summer. My attention was drawn to these fans because the lower sections of the stems fixing them to the ceiling were bright and shiny by comparison with the parts nearest the ceiling which had a much duller appearance. By way of making small talk, I commented on this to the pastor who was showing me round. 'Oh yes,' he said, 'we did that to improve the quality of our praise.' On seeing my bemused look, he went on to explain that these people could do nothing without their hands held high, and in order to encourage them at least to think about why they were doing it, the church leadership had decided to lower the fans to just a little above head height! People can easily do things out of habit in worship, whether it be sitting in serried ranks watching a theatrical-style production from an accomplished ministerial performer, or whether it be in the allegedly more relaxed atmosphere of the kind of church where everything significant happens an arm's length above the heads of the worshippers.

Church number three tries to have the best of all possible worlds by combining practices from the other two. Historically, its people have come from a background where worship was always on the theatrical model, but they would like to learn something from a more exuberant style of worship, and even to incorporate some aspects of it alongside their own traditions. The casual visitor to this congregation would have an interesting experience. The service might begin in what seems to be a very traditional mode, but then part-way through the proceedings a balding man who has been forty-something for as long as anyone can remember, and who obviously regards himself as extraordinarily trendy, appears from the transept and says, 'Now let's have a time of *real* worship'. This is the cue for guitars, drums and other noisy instruments to be dragged out, and a group of musicians (who might easily be the most talented people to do anything through the whole service) then lead 'worship' for ten or fifteen minutes. Here, 'worship' seems to mean singing a particular style of modern praise chorus to the accompaniment of a lot of noisy music. The noisier the better, for it may well be accompanied by much vigorous hand-clapping by the congregation, though probably not much arm-raising. If *this* is worship, then I wonder what had been happening before – and what happens after it? Because typically, the drums and guitars are stacked away again, and the service then continues in the same dreary format as it had before all this started.

As I said, these are caricatures, though most of us will recognize ourselves in them. And not everything about them is bad. Take the theatrical model, for example. The theatre can have a very powerful influence on the lives of those who go to it. My previous description focused on some of the potentially negative aspects of a theatrical-style worship. But there is such a thing as good theatre. Reflect for a moment, though, on what it is that makes for good theatre. It is when it moves from being a mere spectacle that is observed, to engaging with the audience. Theatre moves up a gear when it grabs the attention and the audience get involved. The New Testament gives a similar image of meaningful worship. There, worship seems to be a shared experience, in which everyone has a part, which takes place where people are (rather than up-front on a stage or altar), and has space for all types and ages of people. Like other aspects of the Gospel, worship is intended to be a holistic experience, which engages and uses all the gifts, talents and insights of the whole people of God (and that means more than just the full-time clergy, though it quite definitely includes them too).

There are many ways to define worship. One of my favourites is that worship is all that I am, responding to all that God is. You can think of that in several different ways. Individually, of course, with the emphasis on 'all that *I* am'. Who am I as a person? First and foremost, I am a body: I have a physical dimension. I understand things by touching, seeing, smelling them. I am also a mind, with the capacity to think and reflect on the meaning of things. Then I have feelings and emotions, and relationships which encapsulate yet other dimensions of my complex being. If worship is to engage the whole of myself as an individual, then it will somehow need to include all these facets of the person that I am, and facilitate their response to God.

We can also think of this definition of worship in a corporate dimension. For when people meet together for worship, they are not alone. They meet in the company of others. Who are these others? What would it mean for worship to start from a recognition of 'all that *we* are' together? In any congregation that is even vaguely representative of the whole community, there will be children, young people, older people, women, men, single people, divorced people, married people, blended families, different ethnic backgrounds, various educational backgrounds, people with jobs, people with no jobs ... the possibilities are as endless as the variety of humankind. What would worship need to be like in order to facilitate all these different people responding to God in ways that are meaningful and relevant to them?

Then, of course, God is in there. God is the centre of all worship, and worship would not be worship unless it focused on 'all that God is'. But what is God? That is a big question, and God would not be God without being bigger than anything we can possibly comprehend. But both the Bible and Christian theology provide us with a few signposts. One of the

central confessions of Christianity is that 'the Word became
flesh' (John 1:14). We undermine the heart of the faith if we
try and put it all back into words again. Whatever else it
involves, belief in the incarnation centres on the conviction
that God became a person. If worship is about responding to
all that God is, then relating to persons is going to be a basic
part of it, for the whole of humanity is made 'in God's image'
(Genesis 1:27).

WHAT IS EVANGELIZING WORSHIP?

Worship is fundamental to the Christian life. If worship is a
central part of the Gospel, and if evangelization is about communicating the whole Gospel, then clearly there can be no
effective evangelism without authentic worship. Responding to
the Gospel is about responding to God, and the context in
which this most readily takes place is worship. Maybe that all
sounds somewhat idealistic, for obviously not everything to
which we attach the label 'worship' has a spin-off in effective
evangelization. Churches are worshipping all the time, yet
their numbers still continue to decline throughout the western
world. But the opposite is also true. Churches in other parts of
the world are worshipping all the time – and their numbers are
growing, as their worship attracts people to the reality of God
in their midst. 'Worship is our way to God and at the same
time our celebration of the love of God. The key to authentic
worship is the presence of authentic worshippers.'[7]

What sort of worship, then, will be evangelizing? It would
be easy to answer that question by providing a blueprint indi-
cating how such worship might work out in a particular con-

text. To do so would limit the usefulness of this discussion, for the precise nature of the things people do in worship is culturally relative. But whatever is done should certainly facilitate a holistic response to God. In chapter 2, reference was made to the fact that discipleship ought to engage heart, soul, mind and strength (Mark 12:29–31), and on that minimal definition worship should therefore encompass at least the emotions, thinking and body, as well as having a mystical element to it. If it is to go further, and reflect 'all that we are', then the checklist would soon grow.

In keeping with the purpose of this study, however, we will concentrate on the general attitudes that might inform and inspire evangelizing worship. In this context, it may help if we first identify some of the things that evangelizing worship is not.

1 Worship is not the same as services and meetings

It was Martin Luther who coined the phrase, *Laborare est orare*, 'work is worship'. The early Church would certainly have agreed with him. In the early chapters of Acts, their entire lifestyle is fundamental to the fact that 'day by day the Lord added to their group those who were being saved' (Acts 2:47). The way they related to each other, the style of their meals, their use of material goods: all these things, and others besides, were crucial to their life of evangelization, witness – and worship. The dynamic evangelistic impact of such lifestyles is frequently mentioned in Paul's letters (eg 1 Thessalonians 1:2–10). Everything they did was very public. There were no closed doors in the Church, and that was one of

the things that distinguished them both from their Jewish heritage, and from the many competing sects of the Hellenistic
world. Elsewhere, worship was an event which drew people in
to sacred spaces (temples) at sacred times (religious festivals),
and where scrupulous attention was given to excluding those
deemed to be disqualified from participation. This meant that
in the Jerusalem temple, Gentiles were largely kept out of the
most significant places; in the synagogue, women and children
were strictly separated from the men; and in the many
Hellenistic mystery religions, only initiates were allowed any
access, because by definition everything was kept secret and
hidden from outsiders. But for the earliest Christians, worship
was the reverse of all this. Instead of being an activity requir-
ing withdrawal from the world, the experience of worship
opened them out to the needs and concerns of the world.

This no doubt explains why Christian worship generally
took place in people's homes (Romans 16:3–16, for instance,
lists several 'home churches' that collectively constituted the
Christian community in that city). The typical Roman villa
was both the workplace and the home. Worship and evangelism happened where people lived and worked, and both of
them grew naturally out of the relationships of everyday life.[8]
This inevitably opened up the Church's worship to all sorts of
people, for Christians lived and worked alongside those who
were not yet believers. Their worship needed to display an
uncommon degree of integrity, for home is the one place where
it is impossible to carry on some sort of act. People are most
truly themselves when they are at home.

Much contemporary worship – whether by accident or
design – is exclusive, and caters for those who are already in
the Church. The New Testament implies that worship in the

early Church was an inclusive activity, open to anyone who cared to join it, not just to be a spectator but a participant. Acts describes the Jerusalem Christians worshipping in the street as well as in one another's homes, while Paul took it for granted that unbelievers would be wandering in and out of the worship in the church at Corinth (1 Corinthians 14:24). His description of the setting in which the Eucharist was celebrated is also instructive. In 1 Corinthians 11:23–34, he was seeking to correct abuses of the occasion, caused among other things by rich and prosperous people holding their dinner parties in one corner of the room while poorer people could only sit and watch them. He did not counsel them to abolish this almost festive atmosphere, but instead to correct the injustices and imbalances that were occurring.

New Testament worship also seems to have involved all generations. Children were taken for granted as part of the Church. Modern theological debates about baptism have tended to obscure the sociological fact that the whole structure of the early Church was family-based. If a child belonged in a family, then she belonged to the Church. This is never spelled out categorically simply because it was taken for granted. Nor was it ever a cause of controversy, which explains why it is never formally discussed in any of the New Testament letters (all of which were *ad hoc* responses to particular debates and questions which arose in specific contexts).

The pattern of worship in these early Christian communities explains why no one felt it necessary to establish a Christian temple as an alternative either to the Jerusalem temple, or to the various shrines of other religious traditions. Christians did eventually find themselves conforming to the religious expectations of their pagan neighbours, but this was not the original pattern, and stemmed more from cultural pressures than from the central values of the Gospel.

2 Worship is not something somebody else does for you

Nowadays, it is common to talk of worship as something to be 'conducted' by the clergy or other recognized leaders. Again, this practice did not characterize the life of the early Church. In Corinth, Paul was faced with the problem of what looked like too much participation in worship, as different people within the congregation insisted on doing their own thing — and all doing it at the same time, in competition with one another. This was clearly unsatisfactory, but Paul did not tackle it by insisting they should all be silent while one or two authorized people conducted worship on their behalf. That would have been relatively easy, and in practical terms could well have resolved the problem. But Paul knew that to do so would also have undermined some fundamental aspects of the Gospel itself. So instead of silencing the whole orchestra, he adopted the more difficult course of defining the role of various players, and helping them to get the music in such an order that the end-product would be a harmonious expression of praise to God. In what must be one of the most perceptive essays on worship and ministry in the early Church ever to be written, Ernst Käsemann correctly noted that 'the diversity of charismatic functions is normative even for the ministry of preaching; all ... are bearers of the Word of God and contribute to the edification of the community. Even the apostle is, as Paul is always emphasizing, only one charismatic among many ....'⁹ An insufficient recognition of the importance of this will create a spiritually unhealthy dependency culture in the Church. Whether we realize it or not, people are being taught that being the Church is something somebody else does for them. We will not make effective evangelists that way! It is unrealistic to suppose that people who are not allowed to play a role in the safe environment of the Church will suddenly be able to share their faith in the world outside.

Paul makes exactly the same point more subtly – and more theologically – in his discussion of how the Eucharist should be celebrated. 'Do this ...', he writes (twice, in 1 Corinthians 11 vv 24 and 25), in each case using the *plural* form of the Greek verb for 'do' (*poieite*). For many Christians today, worship is a noun, but for Paul and his contemporaries it was very definitely a verb: a plural verb, as well, because it was to engage the whole Christian community together. No doubt this helps to explain why worship came to be described as 'liturgy'. The Greek word *leitourgia* described the various jobs different citizens carried out in the ideal city-state. These were the things for which they had responsibility and for which they were equipped by their natural gifts and talents. The doing of all these things in harmony with others was what kept the community working properly. Paul's use of the 'body of Christ' image in 1 Corinthians 12:1–31 is a near-perfect application of that into the church context – with one exception. In the Greek city-states, citizens could be forced to play a particular role whether or not they wished to do so. Paul, by contrast, always emphasizes the free and loving service of Christians in response to God's grace. In the New Testament sense, this is what liturgy should be. A 'service' is literally Christians 'serving' one another, as they respond to the greatness and goodness of God. This at once puts a question mark against a theatrical model of worship. If worship is to be service of one another, then by definition this is not something that can happen from the front, regardless of whether it is clergy or lay people who do it. It will take the whole of God's people even to begin to reflect the whole of God's glory to the whole community, and the idea that one or two people can approximate to that – even if they do claim to be expressing themselves on behalf of others – is foreign to scripture. If we cannot be open with one another in church, how can we be open in sharing faith with other people outside it? And if clergy will not be open, weak and vulnerable, why should they expect others to exhibit these characteristics? One of my saddest memories is of a minister with a close relative who had been saved from a disaster in which other people lost their lives, and who insisted that no mention should be made of this in a service, because he would be embarrassed to be prayed for. He himself made a habit of regularly praying for others, of course, and whether or not he realized it, he was sending out signals saying that he had no needs. He did, of course, but by repressing them and keeping everything 'in control' he presumably found it less personally threatening. But in the early Church, 'Let us pray' meant just that (as it does in many churches in the two-thirds world today), not 'You sit still while I pray on your behalf'. Many church leaders wrestle with this, but they frequently give confusing signals, by saying they want others to be 'more involved' in worship, but then never creating any opportunities for them to do so with integrity.

3 Worship is not teaching

The relationship between teaching and worship takes us into a potential minefield, because an over-emphasis on teaching and intellectual learning is a familiar western obsession whose influence extends far beyond the boundaries of the Church. It takes us back to the Enlightenment again, and its stranglehold on the expectations and understandings of western Christianity, particularly the rationalist view that the only things worth knowing are things you can think about. This may well be one key reason why so many churches are on the decline. Some say that the western churches have become very middle-class, but that is questionable. It is more accurate to say that they have become very bookish, and mainly appeal to people who think and process information in particular ways. In worship workshops with churches of many different denominational and theological traditions, I have often used the Honey and Mumford *Learning Skills Questionnaire* as a means of helping people come to terms with what this means both for their worship and their evangelization. Honey and Mumford identify four different learning styles: the Activist, Pragmatist, Reflector and Theorist.[10] I can almost guarantee that any church in the west selected at random will have a substantial preponderance of people who are either reflectors or theorists (most probably the latter). At a time when the numbers of people who prefer these learning styles are declining in the general population (even among the educated middle classes), this is bound to be bad news for the Church's ability to reach other types of people. In so many churches, worship has become a very cerebral activity. Any minister who doubts that could do worse than reflect on how much time is spent on preparation for the various elements of Sunday worship. That will help to identify where our priorities lie, and is likely to be a salutary and challenging experience. It certainly has been for me.

It is a mistake to confuse worship with teaching, and trying to do both at once is likely to mean that we do neither very well, for they are fundamentally different things. The problem is that we have rather taken it for granted that being a Christian is basically a cognitive experience, and so everything needs to be in words all the time. There is nothing wrong with words and thinking, of course: it is all a matter of balance. But it is worth emphasizing this point simply because so many of us have a lop-sided understanding here, and this imbalance affects both the nurture of those who are in the church and the evangelization of those who are not. Sometimes our cerebral bias comes out in simple, even trivial ways. For instance, Christians do not always appreciate how alien things like hard-backed hymn books and Bibles can be to the average person in the street, who in everyday life probably never handles any literature other than a tabloid newspaper and takes in most of their learning from the TV or computer screen. More often, it affects the way we present the Gospel itself. It is not unusual to hear it said that children need to achieve 'years of understanding and/or discretion' in order to make satisfactory faith commitments. Though it might be dressed up to look like theology, that is not essentially a spiritual or theological statement at all. To link faith to a particular level of intellectual attainment or development is a secular rationalist sentiment (and it is, of course, bad news for anyone called to minister to the mentally impaired). This cerebral emphasis has also led to an over-emphasis on the importance of sermons, of children going to Sunday *Schools*, and of teaching, learning, and the assimilation of facts and information generally being of the essence of Christian commitment. Within the Protestant tradition, this all goes back to the Reformation with its insistence on the centrality of 'the word', and it has often been embodied in the stones of church buildings, which are constructed like lecture halls. Their silent message is that people are there to sit and listen, and in many churches it is physically impossible to do anything else.

As I reflect on all this, I find myself challenged – not least because I have spent much of my life thinking, writing about theology, and preaching sermons. It would be convenient if these questions would go away, or could be dismissed as spurious and misguided. But there are at least three pressing reasons why we should take them seriously.

First is an evangelistic concern. Whether we like it or not, it is a simple fact that a cerebral and cognitive approach to faith does not attract ordinary people. When people describe church worship as 'boring' they are not necessarily expressing spiritual preferences. How can they be when all the evidence shows there are far more people engaged in the spiritual search today than ever before? Rather, they are saying, 'This is not my way of doing things – and therefore if this is what Christianity is about, then it's not for me'.

There is also a concern about communication, and the obvious fact that much of what we think is 'teaching' is not getting through anyway. I never cease to be surprised at the numbers of ministers who tell me they have been faithfully teaching their people for years, and yet at the same time bemoan how untaught they are! If that seems to be happening, then no matter what we think has been going on, it obviously was not teaching, because no one has been taught until someone has learned something. And we do not learn all we need to know just by listening. Remember the Chinese proverb: 'I hear – I forget, I see – I understand, I do – I remember.'

In *Finding Faith Today*, John Finney found that many people 'clearly received the Gospel at a non-cerebral level – through human relationships and pastoral care, through mystery, and emotions'. He went on to comment that we need 'means of evangelism which do not rely so heavily upon the communication of a verbal message', and asked, 'Is too much of our evangelizing excessively verbose and aimed only at the intellect?'[11] If mystery and the emotions are part of the ways in which people come to faith, then renewed worship is likely to play a significant part in evangelism. But for worship to be released to do that, we need to recognize that making teaching central is more likely to hinder than to help. American churches generally accept this by holding teaching classes for all ages separately from worship. At least, that is their theory, though in practice 'worship' often turns out to be much the same as teaching, the only difference being the number of hymns and prayers that might be included.

There is also a theological issue involved here. William Abraham comments that 'we need to abandon the image of proclamation that is so prevalent in the modern Protestant tradition. That image, represented by the solid, tripartite sermon, usually read from a manuscript, is a culturally relative phenomenon.'[12] The 'ministry of the word', that has historically been so important to some traditions, can never merely mean teaching the contents of an ancient book. If the concept of 'ministry of the word' is to have any theological integrity, it must imply learning about *the* Word – God's Word – Christ himself. And the way in which 'the Word became flesh' should be a model to modern Christians seeking to encourage others in their faith journeys. The centrality of the incarnation as a model for faith-sharing was touched on in chapter 2, and it is also relevant here. Notwithstanding the sentiments of some of the best-loved Christmas carols, the incarnation is not about how 'God became a man'. At the heart of the Gospel is the fact that 'God became a child', and that makes a world of difference to the models that Christ's disciples are called to adopt in both sharing and celebrating their faith.

The original twelve disciples found it hard to understand why Jesus was not a powerful conqueror, an expert who had everything together, and who simply told people how it was. They struggled not only with the ultimate evidence of his apparent weakness (the cross), but also with his insistence on telling stories and leaving people with personal space to decide for themselves how to respond to his message. This was not their image of how God should work. But it was the medium God chose, and the fourth gospel exhorts its readers to follow God's example in the ways they share their faith (John 20:21). This should also be the model for modern Christians as they seek to evangelize. There is something intrinsically incompatible between the openness of Jesus' style and the way many modern Christians present themselves as 'experts'. Unlike some of today's clergy, Jesus was not 'six feet above contradiction', either literally or metaphorically. He was open to listening to other people, and engaging them in dialogue. We find the same thing in other New Testament books. In Acts 20:7–12, Luke describes Paul's meeting with the Christians in Troas. As a matter of fact, it is the only description anywhere in the New Testament of anything approximating to a church service (as distinct from theoretical advice about worship, of

the sort given, for example, in 1 Corinthians 14:26–40). Most
readers think the significant thing about it was that Paul
spoke until midnight and the unfortunate Eutychus fell
asleep. But what is really interesting here is the way Paul's
'preaching' is described. The NRSV says 'Paul was holding a
discussion with them' (Acts 20:7). The Greek verb used is
dialegomai – the root from which we get the English word
'dialogue'. Paul was 'dialoguing' with these people, listening
as well as speaking (which no doubt explains why he was able
to sustain it for so long). Then later, after the Eucharist had
been celebrated, he 'continued to converse' in a more informal
way until daybreak (Acts 20:11).

A few years ago, I read through all the gospels trying to
identify Jesus' style of evangelization, hoping to find some
guidelines that could be useful today. I was surprised at how
few sermons he preached that were monologues of the sort that
dominate much modern worship. Just counting them all, and
ignoring any questions of duplicate accounts or shared traditions between the various gospels, there are still fewer than
the fingers of one hand. Jesus' weakness and vulnerability is
striking, and evangelists who wish to be as successful as he
was should take a leaf from his book. We have something to
share with others not because we are different, still less
because we are experts, but because we are no different. Their
struggles are our struggles. We share the same tensions of joy
and anger, success and failure, expectancy and frustration.
But however threatening the chaos might be, we also meet
God in it all – and that is really good news (for us as well as
for others).

Teaching and learning can most usefully take place in a
context that is not worship, but that does not mean spoken

communication is wholly inappropriate in worship. After all, if worship is a holistic thing, then that will include verbal messages, albeit combined with many other less cognitive activities. In the context of evangelism, it is worth noting that Christians who are continually criticized in sermons by preachers who pretend they have no problems of their own will not make good evangelists. It takes no skill to overload people with guilt and induce a very low self-esteem. But unless people feel good about themselves and their churches they will never share their faith with others. The same goes for those who come to worship unsure of their faith status: they are likely to be looking for compassion and community, not commitment and challenge. People need to be lifted up, encouraged, enthused and inspired to think it might be worth following Christ – and while there will always be exceptions, the best way to do that is more likely to be through sharing our own stories with one another, than through complex analytical expositions of scripture. That was the style Jesus adopted, and as with so many other things, we could do worse than follow his example.

4 Worship is not all thinking

By the time we reach the age of five, we have already learned more than half of all that we will ever need to know. So think of how a baby learns and discovers things about the world. Eating and tasting seem to be favourite starting points: babies put everything into their mouths, and no matter how much their parents try to discourage it, it will make little difference. Touching and feeling are quite important too – and, eventually we get round to understanding things by thinking. I think it was Kierkegaard who said that you have to live life forwards, and reflect on it backwards: at the end of life, you can perhaps begin to articulate what it has all been about, but at the time you make sense of it in a different way. Now compare this with how we respond to God! Again, our western culture generally warns us off anything to do with the senses. Time and again, we convince ourselves that so far as God is concerned, people cannot trust their feelings: they can only trust theology or the Bible. But why? We trust our feelings everywhere else in life. As a matter of fact, most of us make most of our major life decisions on the basis of our feelings. If we go to buy a car, then the crucial thing is whether it feels right. If we feel happy driving it, we buy it. If not, then regardless of its theoretical specification, we are likely to leave it at the showroom. When we fall in love, the same thing happens, and we decide to form permanent relationships for no other reason than because it feels right. Relating to God is different from relating to a human partner, but it cannot be that different, and if worship truly is all that I am, responding to all that God is, then there is no way that the emotions and feelings can be excluded.

The fact that children were part and parcel of the church in New Testament times should warn us against supposing that its worship was all centred around cerebral activities. If we take seriously the fact that there is an appropriate response to God for different people at different ages and stages of life, we need to accept that some people may never feel the urge to express their faith in theological abstractions, though for others that may easily be a growth point. How many things are there in the average church's worship to engage an individual's total personality? How is the body, and all its senses, engaged in responding to God? How are the emotions caught up, not to mention our human relationships and intuitions? What physical, visible, tangible symbols do we have to direct us to the God whom we come to worship? If the answer is none, then why are we surprised when our churches appeal to only one sort of person, namely those who are able to think and imagine internally in mental abstractions? One of the major reasons for the rapid growth of the New Age in recent years is the need felt by many people for some kind of hands-on symbols, rituals and experiences that will hold out the promise of putting them in tune with the mystery that is God.

There are also a few theological considerations here. If God is really and truly incarnated into our world, then that means Christians should respond to God with all their senses. How do you think Jesus understood and responded to God as a child? If, as the creeds affirm, he was truly and fully divine from the beginning, then that must say something significant about the range and style of our own possibilities.[13] We are impoverished if everything has to be put into words. In human relationships, words are frequently inappropriate or inadequate – so why suppose that words alone could ever be big enough to convey the totality of God's Kingdom? When John the Baptist sent to Jesus wanting to know whether or not he was the Messiah, the response he got was surprisingly non-verbal: 'Go back and tell John what you have seen and heard: the blind receive their sight, the lame walk, the lepers are cleansed, the deaf hear, the dead are raised, the poor have good news brought to them' (Luke 7:22). If worship only addresses our minds, we will be spiritually handicapped – and people who are seriously looking for meaning and direction in life will likely go somewhere else. Contrasting the rising popularity of therapy with the demise of Christianity, one writer

identifies the reason in the fact that Christianity is concerned
with 'dwelling intellectually upon the dogma, with a consequent lack of therapeutic, by which I mean the lack of any
real body of ideas and practices to help people change. The
near total absence of practical aids to human psychological
and spiritual growth within Christianity left a vacuum which
psychotherapy had to fill, based upon principles which it had
to discover for itself.'[14] Exploring the non-rational side of ourselves in a context of worship may at least begin to redress the
balance.

5 Worship should reflect our culture

In both Old and New Testaments, worship was the one point at
which the culture of the day was most strikingly affirmed, and
challenged. In the worship of ancient Israel, mythological stories of monsters and dragons could be rewritten to become
hymns in praise of Israel's own God (eg Psalm 74:12–17). In
the New Testament, baptism (a familiar practice in Judaism as
well as Hellenistic mystery cults) was utilized and given a new
meaning. The familiar was taken up and transcended. In a
very real sense, it was converted! Raymond Fung writes that
worship 'must embrace the everyday concerns of the worshippers. They need to know that the things they care about from
Monday to Saturday, God also cares about.' At the same time
as such worship 'embraces the cares and concerns of our mundane living, it does not deal with them primarily on the level
of human relationships, economics or politics. We do not use
the occasion to indulge in our own political preferences. We
meet to reaffirm our faith in the sovereignty of our great and
compassionate God "who is able to keep us from falling, and

to present us faultless before the presence of his glory with exceeding joy". Such a worship is authentic and, for that very reason, truly evangelistic."[15] It is precisely because Christians are contextualizing their faith within the culture and customs of their own heritage that worship has such a powerful evangelizing dynamic in the world Church today.

The patterns of worship followed by western churches evolved at a time when that was happening in our own culture. Two hundred years ago, most people spent their entire lives in the same community. They travelled only short distances, if at all, and the inhabitants of any particular community not only lived alongside each other, they also worked together and met one another socially every day of the week. What then took place in church on Sundays was a real celebration of their community life, and an opportunity to bless and celebrate what they had done together on the other six days of the week. The kind of services that developed were appropriate expressions of worship for this type of close-knit community. Today, however, that has all gone. The average church does not reflect the life of a recognizable community, because people now travel more and work at a distance from where they live. Even a parish church is likely to be a gathered church in this sociological sense. As a result, the church finds itself saddled with patterns of celebration that no longer reflect contemporary culture and lifestyles, and so it is unable effectively to challenge and transform them. Instead of Sunday worship blessing and celebrating the activities of the rest of the week, what happens in church is radically different from everyday life, even as it is lived by those who belong to the church! Today's churches may first need to build community before it can be celebrated. This chapter has highlighted the holistic

nature of true worship, as something that should engage the
whole of God's people using the whole of their faculties to
respond to the greatness of God. Since most of us are already
quite good at engaging our minds in worship, we will probably
need to work hard at identifying appropriate ways of engaging
our bodies and our emotions. In their book *Megatrends 2000*,
sociologists John Naisbett and Patricia Aburdene confirm that
this is in any case one of the major concerns of our culture,
and they predict that interest in the creative and visual arts
will take over from involvement in sport as a major leisure
activity of the next decade.[16] This is a major cultural peg on
which evangelizing worship can quite easily be hung by those
with spiritual vision.

The *Epistle to Diognetus*, a second-century apologetic
explaining and commending Christianity, lays considerable
emphasis on the fact that Christians were fully a part of the
culture of the time: 'The difference between Christians and
the rest of humankind is not a matter of nationality, or language, or customs. Christians do not live apart in separate
cities of their own, speak any special dialect, or practise any
eccentric way of life.' The anonymous author goes on to affirm,
however, that they do 'have some features that are remarkable', foremost among them the fact that 'for them, any foreign
country is a motherland, and any motherland is a foreign
country.'[17] Striking the right balance between accepting the
secular community as our 'motherland', and yet questioning
its values as part of 'a foreign country' is both demanding and
essential for any effective evangelization. Part of the challenge
involves accepting the ethos of our culture. Some years ago I
wrote an article for a popular magazine under the title *Real
Churches have Organs*, in which I discussed the unease some

have in utilizing culturally appropriate musical instruments in the context of worship. It obviously struck chords with many readers, and produced the largest postbag I have ever had. Considering some of the (to me) more interesting things I have written on other topics, that in itself probably says something about the points at which many churches find themselves wrestling with culture. It somehow seems easier to live with what Michael Marshall aptly calls 'the claustrophobia of religiosity', than it is to interact creatively with culturally appropriate ways of doing things.[18]

It is not just in terms of the content of services that we need to think through our culture more profoundly. What about the times at which Christians meet for worship? One of the reasons why more people went to church in previous generations is that what the church did fitted their overall lifestyle more closely than tends to be the case today. The times at which churches met on late Sunday mornings related to an agricultural economy in which farmers needed to structure their day around the milking times of cows. Then when gas lighting was invented, churches started to meet on Sunday evenings, though not too late because in those early days technology was insufficiently advanced to guarantee the reliability of safe lighting, either in church buildings or in the street. In any case, with little organized public transport people needed to allow plenty of time to walk home. And so began the hallowed traditions – still followed in many churches – of meeting each Sunday at 11 am and 6.30 pm. A friend of mine was invited to preach at a church whose services were at 11.10 am and 6.10 pm, and thinking these were somewhat curious times he asked why. The answer was simple: people used to catch the train to the church, and it arrived at the nearby station five minutes past each hour. The railway track to that particular town had been inoperational since the 1930s, yet the church still continued to meet at times convenient for rail travellers half a century earlier! When we compare the Sunday habits of Christians with the demands faced by other people, it is not hard to see why so many simply cannot fit church into their schedule. Many people find that Sunday is the only time available for a whole variety of significant tasks. They visit relatives, do the shopping, engage in recreational activities of one sort and another, and spend time just being together. To be relevant, the church needs to take account of all this, instead of sticking with outmoded habits which not only sideline those not in the church, but also impose an enormous load of guilt on their own members, whose lifestyle also requires them to do these things on Sundays, and somehow fit church in as well. Churches could do worse than take a fresh look at all this, and some might even want to ask if Sunday really is the best time to meet anyway.

Our culture also has a spirituality of its own, expressed most obviously in the thinking we now identify as the New Age, but also more widely. Most Christians have been programmed to think that God always works in neatly definable ways in people's lives. Different Christians will have different ideas of what those ways are, depending on their own traditions: they know a person is on a 'real' spiritual search when they look and sound the same as them. But God's Spirit does not always work that way, and many Christians are unable to perceive where God is at work because of their own limited expectations. One of the great ironies of our time is the way that the western churches are declining at the same time as the sense of spiritual search in the community is increasing in intensity and fervour. When we begin to see the world the way God sees it, we might be able to accept other people's starting points, and welcome them into the worshipping community.

It is easy to dismiss all this as peripheral to the business of evangelization. But to do so is a mistake – and the experience of growing churches all over the world shows it to be. It is unrealistic – and certainly theologically and biblically hetero-dox – to separate the renewal of worship from the evangelistic task. This may well be the key question to which the western churches need to address themselves today. What happens in worship could well turn out to be the single most influential factor in our success – or failure – as evangelists.

Sigmund Freud once saw a patient who tried to convince him she had a happy marriage, while all the time she was slipping her wedding ring on and off her finger. When real problems later surfaced, he remembered this and realized that her unconscious body language conveyed a more accurate message than the words she used. Much evangelization seems to be like this. Christians are trying to convince others of the truth of their message, while in terms of their own experience of worship they are slipping the ring on and off their fingers. Renewed worship will not only attract outsiders. It will also equip and empower those who are already committed to Christ.

There are plenty of resources available within the Christian tradition to enable worship to become truly evangelizing, empowering people to respond in the totality of their being to all that God is. Historically, different sections of the Church have highlighted different details, as if they were the complete picture. One of the encouraging outcomes of today's increased ecumenical awareness is the appreciation that different traditions can enrich one another, learn from one another, and together move to a new position. Historically, the sacramental understanding of worship has emphasized signs, symbols, ikons and so on, and in its own way has focused on the non-cognitive side of worship. But it has generally played down the importance of learning and beliefs, and as a result has often degenerated into empty ritual. The evangelical tradition, on the other hand, has majored on the importance of theological understanding, and the centrality of preaching. It has minimized the significance of feelings, and all too often has produced an arid and narrow Biblicism, confusing scriptural knowledge with love of God. As a consequence, it lacks the power to challenge or transform the will and redeem the emotions. The charismatic approach has unhesitatingly gone for the need of people to be moved and healed by worship – often to the neglect of any serious reflection on the meaning of faith. As a result, it can become little more than a form of subjective personal therapy. Each one of these traditions has identified some things that are central to the concept of evangelizing worship. But the potential richness of worship only becomes apparent when all three combine. One of the greatest Old Testament characters, Isaiah, was called to be a prophet through such an experience, and the account of his call specifically identifies the characteristics of sacramental, evangelical and charismatic worship as having a part to play (Isaiah 6:1–8). Authentic worship still inspires the prophetic vision and attracts people to follow Christ, because it opens new windows onto God's glory and goodness, and provides a holistic context in which the whole of the human personality can begin to respond to everything that God is. And that, surely, is what evangelism is all about.

chapter six | Evangelizing Strategies for the Local Church

Once congregations begin to realize the need for sharing their faith with other people, they are easily fired up with visionary enthusiasm. As we consider the development of various international movements for evangelization throughout the 20th century, there is no shortage of rhetoric to encourage us to think big as we contemplate the evangelistic task. Back in 1910, John Mott enthused the Edinburgh International Missionary Conference with his talk of 'the evangelization of the world in this generation'. Eighty years later, the sloganizing was still going on, as the Lausanne II International Congress on World Evangelization met in Manila, under a banner which spoke confidently of how they would equip 'the whole Church to take the whole Gospel to the whole world'.[1]

There are several biblical passages which can provide inspiration for this kind of grand vision. When Paul gave an account of his own ministry to the court of Herod Agrippa II, he spoke in the same style (Acts 26:16–18), and by any standards his achievements were remarkable. For the striking language he used to explain the nature of his evangelistic calling was matched by his ability in being able to deliver the goods. Paul was perhaps the most successful Christian evangelist there has ever been. In less than a generation he travelled the length and breadth of the Mediterranean world, establishing growing and active Christian communities wherever he went. He and others of his generation not only spoke of changing the world with the Gospel: they quite literally did that.

So what was their secret? Paul, of course, was always conscious that he was only a messenger, and that it was the power of the Spirit which really brought a change to the lives of those whom he met. It is easy for us to look back with rose-tinted spectacles, knowing as we do that Paul's enterprise was successful. But in reality, things were no easier for him than they had been for Jesus a generation earlier. As he considered the many hardships he had to endure, he described himself as a 'common clay pot', just a temporary container for the renewing power of God, which was the real source of his success (2 Corinthians 4:7). Running throughout the story of these earliest Christian communities is the conviction that the great expansion of the Church was the work of God. In chapter 3 it was suggested that what God is doing in the world must always be primary in our thinking on evangelism: 'God's Story', as it was called there. The first Christians knew that. They were such unlikely people to change the world, it was obvious that if anything was going to happen, it would not be through their own efforts. But they began with the certain knowledge that because God was at work, literally anything could happen. That undoubtedly gave a cutting edge to their witness to faith in Jesus Christ, and is absolutely foundational for understanding their success.

PLANNING FOR SUCCESSFUL EVANGELISM

At the same time, however, they never made the mistake of thinking that even heavenly visions could come to fruition by themselves, without some hard thinking and incisive planning. Paul is a classic example of a mission strategist, and the careful design and planning of his own work shines through, both in the book of Acts and in his own writings. There is no question that Paul was excited by the possibility of spreading the Gospel through the whole of the Mediterranean basin in his own lifetime. He was a fanatic in the true sense of the word! But he also knew that for this vision to become reality, he would need to give careful thought as to how it could be done. The great visionary and idealistic aims were important: they would motivate him to the very end of his days. But bringing them to fruition required him to identify a series of specific goals, and then to develop strategies that would enable him to achieve what he wanted to do. Appreciation of this is going to be important for Paul's modern-day successors. Most of us tend to be good on ideals and aims, and not so good on goals and strategy. This is often for the best reasons, of course: we feel the urgency of the task, and in the face of enormous need we assume that time spent in prayerful planning will be time wasted. Why waste time praying, reading books (the Bible included), attending workshops and conferences, listening to the experience of other Christians, when we could be out there getting on with the job? It is tempting to think that way. But it is the pathway to personal frustration, institutional disintegration, and spiritual ineffectiveness. If that had been Paul's attitude, the chances are he would have

worn himself to a standstill in no time at all, and ended his
life in despair with the task still uncompleted. As it was, he
knew the value for evangelism of listening, as well as speaking: listening to God, to other Christians, and to the
unchurched culture in which he ministered. Because he
understood the importance of that, we are still in awe of his
achievements two thousand years later. These are skills that
today's evangelists must also learn to excel in.

There can be no question that Paul's meeting with the Lord
on the Damascus road was a crucial turning point in his life. It
challenged his personal priorities, not to mention his theology,
and according to all the accounts, he was specifically conscious on that occasion of receiving a call to evangelize the
world (Acts 9:15, 22:15, 26:16–20; Galatians 1:11–12,
15–16). By the time his sight had been restored, he knew for
certain that his life would never be the same again, and it
would be spent in sharing the good news about Jesus. Within a
few days of his arrival in Damascus, that was exactly what he
was doing, in the streets and the synagogues and anywhere
else that people would listen. He had all the verve and energy
of a new convert, and a burning desire to spread his message
far and wide. His commitment and enthusiasm were at a high
point. Surely, he must have been tempted to launch out immediately in pursuance of the missionary task that was to be his
life's work. In fact, Paul did the exact opposite. In the short
term, he withdrew from public life and went off into the desert
near Damascus to work through his new experience, and, no
doubt, to reflect on the best way of approaching the enormous
task that now lay before him (Galatians 1:17). Even after that,
Paul eased himself into it only slowly. It was three full years
before he had any contacts with the original church back in

Jerusalem, and it was another fourteen years after that when he found himself heading to Jerusalem as part of an official delegation from the church in Antioch.[2] At that time, Paul had only recently arrived there, having been brought to that Syrian city just a year or so earlier to facilitate the work of this largely gentile congregation. There is a good deal of disagreement as to how these time periods of three and fourteen years relate to each other, but there is no question that it was well over a decade after his Damascus road experience before Paul had the opportunity to put his strategy for evangelism into operation.[3]

In describing Paul's planning procedure, a few technical terms have been used and it will be worthwhile unpacking them a little. First of all, Paul had a great visionary aim. That was what motivated and inspired him: the grand vision. But then by way of fulfilling this grand vision he set up a series of specific goals. These were particular tasks that were not themselves the grand vision, but which would all contribute to the implementation of the broader mission statement. Then he adopted a series of strategies in order to move towards the achievement of those goals: the detailed things that would need to happen to get from A to B. For a simple example of this, we might think of how towards the end of his missionary travels Paul took a collection to help the church in Jerusalem. He knew the Jerusalem church was suffering financial hardship, and he had this great idea that all the gentile churches he had established in Greece and Asia Minor could send a gift to them as an expression of love and solidarity. At the back of his mind there was also the hope that such an act of generosity would help to smooth over the problems that some Jewish believers felt about accepting Gentiles directly into the church without insisting they should all become Jews first (Romans 15:25–28). This was definitely the grand vision: a sharing of resources, and the strengthening of worldwide Church unity. It is the sort of vision that is easy to dream about for a long time (give or take a few details, it is an ideal that the world Church today still strives for). But before such a dream can become reality, specific goals need to be set. Paul did that. He set a goal that was specific in terms of its objective (he would personally take the collection to Jerusalem), and also in terms of its time-scale: he would be there by the Day of Pentecost (Acts 20:16). When the Day of Pentecost came, Paul was able to know for sure whether or not he had made it. To maximize the chances of success, however, he also needed an appropriate strategy. And so he set specific targets for members of the churches as they gave their contributions (1 Corinthians 16:1–4), and during the process he arranged for reports showing how it was going (2 Corinthians 8:16–24). He also seems to have delegated other people to co-ordinate the effort in churches with which he himself had no immediate physical contact, and Troas was the central collection point where they all met up before proceeding to Jerusalem (Acts 20:4–6), no doubt because that was a regular embarkation point for the sea passage that could get them to Palestine by the deadline date. But in the midst of all this planning, the grand vision had not been displaced: it continued to inspire people to give, and they often did so beyond their means and disregarding the urgency of their own needs (2 Corinthians 8:1–5).[4]

Paul used exactly the same planning process in his evangelistic work. He had to, because it was going to be an uphill struggle to spread the Christian message right across the

Mediterranean world in the course of his lifetime. He was realistic about the opposition he would face, and the built-in barriers to the Gospel that the Roman Empire presented. Potentially, racism could have been an enormous problem. Though Jewish people contributed a great deal to the economic success of the empire, they were still the objects of suspicion, if not hatred, by those who held the reins of power.[5] The possibility of class conflict also loomed large, because to be faithful to Jesus his followers needed to be open to all sorts of people, including slaves – and that would immediately place the Church in situations of potential confrontation with the economic system of the day. Quite apart from social barriers of this kind, the empire was a very pluralistic culture, with many religious faiths competing for attention. Under the onslaught of philosophical speculations, the old religions of Greece and Rome had lost their power to attract, but philosophy had not taken their place in the popular imagination. As a result, there was a great spiritual vacuum at the heart of the empire, and religious practices of all kinds were rushing in to try and fill it.[6] Moreover, within this market-place of faiths the Church was less well organized than most of its competitors. By comparison with the population of the empire, its numbers were small, it had no real structure, few if any full-time professional Christian workers, and those it did have were (with only few exceptions) generally not the kind of people who were naturally equipped to make a big impact on society.

Paul was not operating in some privileged situation. The challenges facing him were no easier than those faced by the Church today, and in some ways they were a good deal more complex and demanding. In the light of that, how then did he manage to make such extraordinary progress? First, he made the effort to understand the culture in which he operated, its strengths as well as its weaknesses. He was also prepared to use his culture, and exploit to the full the opportunities that gave him in terms of his mission. But then he also addressed his message quite specifically to the needs of his culture, whether they were moral and spiritual or social and economic.

Once he began to understand his culture, he soon realized that in terms of the successful completion of his mission, he had a lot going for him. There was the universal use of the Greek language, for instance. Ever since the time of Alexander the Great, Greek had been the international language of the Mediterranean world. That meant Paul, as a native Greek speaker, could travel anywhere in the empire and be easily understood. Moreover, it meant he could write in Greek to people in distant cities, and his letters could be read without the need for translation.[7] Even the spiritual vacuum of his day presented creative opportunities, for the collapse of traditional western religious traditions was accompanied by an increasing curiosity about religions originating in the east. In terms of the empire, that meant the faiths of Palestine (Judaism and Christianity), as well as esoteric cults from places like Egypt and Persia. So the real question over which Paul had to strategize was how best to organize his own itinerary in such a way that he would achieve maximum geographical coverage with his message.

Paul's route was never haphazard. He can rightly be described as a frontier evangelist, yet he never visited a geographical frontier himself. He could have spent months, even years, trekking through uncharted territory, or picking his way laboriously across country paths to reach remote places. He did neither of these things. Instead, he took advantage of the major highways the Romans had built across their empire. Combined with regular sea routes, they gave ready access to all the major centres of population, and these were the places Paul visited. Trade and distribution were organized on a provincial basis, and the capital cities of the Roman provinces were crucial hubs of communication, for Paul as for the many merchants who were constantly on the move. Paul made a conscious decision to go in person to those places that were easy to reach, and would be key centres of communication. He knew that he could never personally take the Gospel to every person throughout the empire. But if he was able to establish enthusiastic groups of Christians in the capital cities, then they in turn could spread the good news into more remote areas. Moreover, visitors from rural districts were always travelling into their nearest urban centre, to market their goods in exchange for things they needed back home. If these people were reached with the Gospel, then they would take their faith back to their own people. At least one of the churches to which Paul subsequently wrote a New Testament letter (Colossae) was the product of this strategy, and had been evangelized by Epaphras, one of Paul's converts in Ephesus, which was the capital of the province of Asia. But there would be others, and it is likely that many of the people Paul identifies as his co-workers were engaged in this sort of church planting exercise.

EVANGELISM AND LOCAL CULTURE

Martin Luther once observed that 'If you preach the Gospel in all aspects with the exception of the issues which deal specifi-

cally with your time, you are not preaching the Gospel at all.'[8]
For Paul, doing this effectively involved three things.

Building Bridges

As Paul reflected on the need for persuasive communication,
he never made the mistake of thinking that one person was
pretty much the same as another. This is one of the factors to
which we need to give urgent attention today. Modern
Christians tend to assume that the Gospel can be articulated
in exactly the same way no matter to whom we are trying to
communicate. Naturally enough, we unconsciously imagine
that everyone is like us, and so we angle our evangelization
towards a particular kind of person. Of course, people like us
need to hear the Gospel. But there are specific issues that
need to be addressed in different cultures. The key issues
change from one generation to another, and the questions of
people today are quite different from the questions of people
in our grandparents' generation. They will also be different for
different groups within the community. We have already identified some of today's leading questions in chapter 2, but it
will not do simply to adopt someone else's understanding: we
need to be ready to listen to the actual people we meet, and
formulate our message accordingly.

Take just two examples from the New Testament, both of
them documented in Acts 14. When Paul got to the city of
Iconium in the southern part of the Roman province of
Galatia, he found there a large Jewish population (Acts
14:1–7). Most of the cities he visited had significant Jewish
communities. For these people, the Hebrew scriptures were
their rule of life, and the synagogue was the focal point of their

community. Like Jews everywhere, they were looking forward to the fulfilment of the ancient promises, and eagerly awaiting the appearance of the Messiah who would usher in God's Kingdom. With people like this, Paul had a head start. Their culture had already raised all the questions to which Paul thought he knew the answers. And they were asking those questions in terms with which Paul was familiar, for he too came from a Jewish background in a great Hellenistic city. They did not always accept what he said, but the content of Paul's message was in no doubt: Jesus was the Messiah for whom they were waiting. The synagogues were also a good place to contact non-Jewish people, especially the upper classes. Many thinking gentile people were attracted to the Jewish faith, partly because of its ancient roots, partly also because it offered them a more structured moral framework than their own *laissez-faire* society provided. Some of them accepted the Jewish faith, and became full proselytes by being circumcised and keeping the whole of the Old Testament Law. Others were referred to as 'God fearers', sharing the religious values of Judaism but unwilling to take upon themselves the burden of keeping the Law. Wherever there was a synagogue, Paul always headed there first. Not only did he meet people like himself (and, like us, he felt more at home with them than anywhere else), but he was also likely to meet significant people in the gentile community. Paul knew well enough that the Gospel had a special place for the poor and marginalized. But he also recognized the importance of reaching the decision-makers and property owners. The synagogue was a good place to start doing that.

The city of Lystra was just to the south-west of Iconium, but it was a totally different sort of place. It was geographically off

the beaten track, and was also a Roman colony: a place that
had been settled by Roman citizens, mostly veterans from the
imperial army. Their colony was established about 6 BC at the
instigation of Augustus, who wanted to consolidate his power
in the province of Galatia. There would be a minimal Jewish
population in a place like this, and quite different ways of
looking at things. They certainly had no interest in the Old
Testament, and probably no knowledge of it at all. Nor (unlike
the people whom Paul later met in Athens, Acts 17:16–34)
did they have any acquaintance with the theories of the Greek
philosophical schools. Their spirituality was altogether more
straightforward, and centred on devotion to the traditional
Greek pantheon. People like this were not going to be attracted by a sermon on the identity of the Messiah (that would have
meant nothing to them), nor by an apologetic lecture on philosophical themes (that would have been over their heads). The
thing that spoke to them was the healing of a man who was
lame, as a result of which Paul had an opportunity to tell them
more of the Christian faith (Acts 14:8–20).[9]

There is much that we could learn from these (and other)
stories of Paul's evangelizing strategy. We need to remember
that culture is not a national characteristic, but a local phenomenon. Even in the same town, there will be several different cultures, each with their own questions and potential entry
points for the Gospel. Many churches assume that geography
is a useful way of defining culture. This is the basis on which
the parish structure originated, and it can easily mean that a
single church might find itself with two or three (even more)
quite distinct cultures within a single parish. We will need to
be very flexible to relate to them all, and prepared to adopt
different styles for different types of people. We also need to

beware of the tyranny of 'the good idea', a strategy that works well in somebody else's parish. What is a good idea in one church is neither more nor less than that: a good idea for that one church. It is unlikely to be an effective strategy for another church, because there will be distinctive cultural factors that have contributed to its success in that particular place, and other cultural factors that will tend to undermine its usefulness in a different place. This is why it makes more sense for us to share our attitudes to evangelism, rather than our blueprints. It might seem easier to pick up a ready-made plan from somewhere else, but in the long run it is likely to lead to frustration and bewilderment, as we invest a lot of time, energy and money, and still reap very meagre results. To be sensitive to the needs of the actual people to whom we minister will take more effort (and, I daresay, more spiritual discernment), but that is the only way to anchor the Gospel in our own culture.

Getting Alongside People

We have previously noted the importance of effective two-way communication in the evangelistic task. Like Jesus, Paul exemplifies this in the way he seeks to get alongside people. If evangelism is to be successful, we must start where people are, not just in terms of place, but also in terms of their own thinking and understanding. In the earlier discussion of conversion we saw how Paul has been misunderstood as a result of being viewed through the experience of Martin Luther. But this is not the only distortion in modern perceptions of Paul. A false image of Paul has been created in the likeness of nineteenth-century western imperialism, and he has been unjustly caricatured as the ultimate exponent of an oppressive and unappealing style of evangelization. It is undeniable that some of the worst excesses of Protestant missions in the last two hundred years have claimed to find their inspiration in Paul, perceiving him as an abrasive retailer, purveying a pre-packaged religious product wherever he could find consumers gullible enough to buy it. This is, at best, a one-sided view of Paul, if not a complete misunderstanding of all that he stood for. The book of Acts and Paul's letters speak with a common voice at this point. Paul was not motivated by the mentality of the enterprise culture, driven by the desire for successful empire-building. On the contrary, his style of faith-sharing was so relaxed that he was constantly surprised at the extraordinary results it produced – something to which the thanksgiving sections of his letters frequently testify.

Paul's method was not a form of megaphone diplomacy, nor was it based on authoritarian principles, and he always spoke *with* people rather than *at* them. Whether in the synagogue or, as at Ephesus, in a hired lecture hall, Paul was always open to challenge and debate (Acts 19:8–10), and when he describes his own evangelistic procedures in 1 Thessalonians 2:1–12, he goes to some lengths to emphasize that he was not interested in bullying people to make them accept his message. Paul can on occasion use military metaphors, but when he writes of evangelization he uses the language of the nursery, not of the battlefield. His concept of sharing of the Gospel began from the expectation that he would need first to share himself (1 Thessalonians 2:5–12). By so doing, he created a space in which other people could also be themselves, and decide without coercion how and when to respond to the challenge of the Gospel. Paul adopted the same open-ended approach with

his converts, and it is obvious that many of the profound
heartaches that emerge in his letters stemmed from his practice of allowing and encouraging converts to develop their own
sense of spiritual maturity, rather than imposing a ready-made
framework on them.[10] We desperately need to learn from Paul
at this point.

Developing Right Attitudes

In terms of his own expectations, Paul always thought posi-
tively. Because he began from the premise that God is at work
anyway, he was able to expect things to happen – and so he
knew it was worth taking the risk of challenging people to follow Jesus. Like Jesus, Paul was able to challenge people
effectively, because he was doing it from alongside them, and
from a position of personal vulnerability and openness, rather
than a position of strength. His model was not a sergeant-
major, trying to boss people into the Kingdom, but 'a nurse,
tenderly caring for her own children' (1 Thessalonians 2:7).
Does this indicate part of the reason for our own ineffectiveness? Could it be that we often get no results because we
never ask for anything? Maybe even that we are not in a credible position from which we could invite others to discipleship?
Are we content to allow people to circulate on the fringes of
the Church without looking for specific commitments? And
are we unable to challenge without threatening them, because
we are not ourselves prepared to be open to their needs and
questions?

Stagnating churches are often the victims of their own attitudes. They always think negatively. Someone shares a new
insight or idea, and before they have even finished explaining

it, a dozen people will have thought of fifty good reasons why
it won't work. We can be defeated by ourselves, long before we
start to engage with others! We think small because we have
small expectations of God. Paul could think big because he
knew he was in the service of a big God. William Carey got it
right with his slogan, 'Attempt great things for God – expect
great things from God'.

These then were the factors that led to Paul's establishment
of strong, growing churches, which had mission at their heart.
They were churches that grew naturally, as people were
attracted to what they found in them. They were churches that
had no need to recruit evangelists to lead missions: that only
makes sense in a church where mission is an event. These
churches were more concerned to develop people whose whole
lifestyle would be directed towards the activity of mission.
Here, evangelism was a natural part of the pastoral process,
and every member of the congregation was mobilized for the
task of sharing the good news. That is how Jesus expected it to
be. The new command 'that you love one another' encouraged
his followers to believe that 'by this everyone will know that
you are my disciples' (John 13:34–35). 'Jesus made it
absolutely clear that Christians who love one another in unity
are capable of proving to the world the divine nature of
Christian fellowship and the deity of Jesus Christ ... The new
command is a missionary command. The command to love one
another is not a domestic policy of the church. It is its foreign
policy. It is, if we like, a missionary position ... '¹¹ Taking
evangelization seriously will have far-reaching implications
for the way we worship. It will also place new constraints on
the way we structure our church communities.

PROFILE OF AN EVANGELIZING CHURCH

In several of his writings, Michael Green has identified the church at Antioch as a model church in this respect.[12] It was certainly one of the most outstandingly successful missionary churches mentioned in the New Testament, 'the cradle of Christianity'.[13] This was the first place where significant numbers of Gentiles became Christians, as the Gospel was presented in culturally appropriate ways. It was here too that the followers of Jesus were first given the name 'Christians' (Acts 11:26). Moreover, Antioch was Paul's home church, the congregation from whom he received all his inspiration, and much of his support. It will be worthwhile to reflect on some of the characteristics of this church.

Open to One Another – and to the World

We saw in the previous chapter how worship is something that all God's people are called on to do together. But the church in Antioch appears to have been structured along similar lines, with a plural and diverse leadership. In Acts 13:1, five people are listed as leaders in this church, and they are an interestingly diverse bunch: 'Barnabas, Simeon who was called Niger, Lucius of Cyrene, Manaen a member of the court of Herod the ruler, and Saul.' Barnabas we know to have been a landowner from Cyprus (Acts 4:36–37). Simeon is described as 'Niger', which most likely means he was an African. Manaen was quite probably a childhood companion of Herod Antipas. We know nothing of Lucius, and then there was Saul, a fairly well-off Hellenistic Jew. They obviously were not all from the same social class or educational and racial background. Nor were they the only leaders in the church. Two more are named in Acts 15:32, but who knows how many there were in total? This looks very much the sort of church which led Ernst Käsemann to claim that in the New Testament 'all the baptized are "office-bearers"... [which] seems to be as good as saying that really none of them are.'[14] It is also consistent with the way in which Paul – as an apostle – was easily able to

Youth Fellowship
Bible Study/Prayer
Commitment
Deacons
Priest
GOD
Minister
Elders
Register
S.S
Men's group
Women's group
ROL
P.C.C.
Members
Adherents
Sunday congregation

Youth Club
Weddings
Funerals
B.B
Mother & Toddler
baptisms
dedications
S.S

Static   Closed doors   Under siege
Inward-looking   'Strong'
Defensive   Unchanging   'In the world
                                        but not of it . . .'

accept the ministry even of his own converts. Consider, for example, the way he describes his Philippian converts as 'partners', rather than subordinates, emphasizing that they have had this status right from the very first day when they came to faith (Philippians 1:3–6).

Historically, the churches with which most of us are familiar have tended to be run like business organizations or governments, with a management structure that starts at the top and extends downwards. In this kind of organization, decisions are taken by those who are in charge. Policy is determined in relationship to the way they perceive the needs of the structure, and the fewer people who take part in the decision-making process, the more smoothly things appear to run. At the time of the Industrial Revolution, most businesses operated this way. In the work-place it led to a mechanistic structure, in which workers were treated as if they were replaceable machine-parts, rather than as individuals with any worthwhile personal insights or objectives. Churches are not the same as commercial enterprises. They are voluntary service organizations, which people choose to join, or not to join as the case may be. Here, the top-down style of leadership tends to have a different outcome. Unlike workers, church members cannot be ordered to carry out certain tasks, and as a result most of the real work ends up being done by those who are in charge.[15]

Of course, all that is changing today. 'The mechanistic, reductionist Enlightenment paradigm that has dominated the school, workplace, church and mission for the last 250 years is breaking down. The full shape of the new paradigm is not yet clear. It is likely to be biological rather than mechanical, relational rather than individualistic, systemic rather than reductionistic, and integrated as opposed to dichotomistic. This means we need new kinds of leaders, thinking about the world in new ways ... '[16] In this new atmosphere, the balance of responsibility has shifted, and management strategists might talk of an organization belonging to its 'stakeholders', that is 'all those inside or outside an organization who are directly affected by what it does'.[17] In industrial terms, 'stakeholders' might include such groups as employees, suppliers, investors, consumers, the government, and so on. The objectives of a corporation conceived in this way would be '*not* to serve any one of its stakeholder groups to the exclusion of any of the others. *It is to serve all of them by increasing their ability to pursue their objectives more efficiently and effectively.*'[18]

This raises two significant questions for the church, both of them related to the evangelistic task. Who are the leaders? and Who are the stakeholders? To take leaders first, there is no doubt that closed church structures of the kind where the leaders' main role is to take all the decisions about what needs to be done, and then carry them through themselves, will tend to stymie effective mobilization of our human resources. Because of the rapid changes in our culture, this structure is becoming less and less capable of doing anything at all, but inasmuch as it can still be made to work, it is geared up for maintenance and not for mission. It is virtually impossible for a church organized this way to be a church with mission at the centre.

It is not so long ago that people expected to find their own worth through paid employment. This is no longer an option, partly as a result of rising unemployment, partly through increased dissatisfaction with a materialist worldview. There is already evidence of the adoption of 'designer lifestyles', as people put work lower down their personal agenda, and rate personal fulfilment correspondingly higher. Over the next few years, change in this direction is likely to accelerate very quickly.[19] As people look around for ways to maximize their usefulness, they will increasingly want to belong, to be a part of things, to have a contribution to make. If they have no opportunity to do so, then much of the corporate energy of the church will be taken up with its own internal tensions. Leaders who continue to hold onto the old 'top-down' style will increasingly find themselves feeling like the cork in a well-shaken bottle of champagne – and the fewer people there are in the cork, the greater the tensions are likely to be. Unfortunately, there is always the danger that the cork will be blown out, probably blown apart, and the precious contents of the bottle wasted. At the same time as old-style leaders find it tougher to hold on, other Christians who are committed to the church will find themselves facing increasing pressures as they wrestle with irreconcilable tensions between the Gospel, with its promise of new life (which matches their personal aspirations), and their experience of ecclesiastical structures which seem to have the opposite effect. Some of them may leave: it is not hard to resign from a group where there are no real relationships of mutual acceptance and affirmation. At the same time – and tragically – unchurched people who are engaged in the spiritual search are likely to look in from the outside to such churches, and see what they offer as irrelevant to their own primary desire to make as much of their life as they possibly can, by being useful to others as well as to themselves. In terms of evangelism, the difference between the traditional model and the stakeholder model is the difference between a church still trying to package and market a reli-

gious product which people may take if they want (they typically don't), and offering the Gospel – which will change us as
well as them. The one battens down the hatches, seeing itself
as a faithful remnant under siege, possibly even regarding
itself as 'strong' because it refuses to change. But this kind of
inward-looking and defensive church will never evangelize.
The other might be regarded as doctrinally 'weak' because it
networks into the community, its structures are flexible, and it
is geared towards building bridges to people who are not yet
believers. But it takes seriously the challenge of Jesus' question, 'Who are my friends?' (Matthew 12:46–50) – and is
effective in reaching people with the good news.

So much for the church's leaders. But who do we mean by
the 'stakeholders' in the church? The answer to that would
vary from one congregation to another. But people in my list
would be God, the members of the church, their friends and
relatives, youth groups, Sunday Schools, clergy, lay leaders,
people's work contacts, those who attend the church, groups
such as parent and toddler groups, and the general public.
Though he has not used the same terminology, Raymond Fung
has pointed the way to how such a model of church can be
evangelizing, by entering into partnerships with people of
goodwill in the community, and on that basis being account-
able to the 'stakeholders' and bearing witness to 'the hope that
is within us' (1 Peter 3:15).[20] The way this might work would
be for a church to identify the other people working in its
patch, with a concern to meet the needs of the same people.
Many of these people will be working with a vision statement
that is at least amenable to Christian values, if not based on
them: the 'Isaiah Vision' in Raymond Fung's definition. A
town-centre church, for instance, might identify dentists,

GOD

MOTHERS AND
TODDLERS

MEMBERS

FRIENDS/
RELATIVES

MINISTER

CHURCH

SUNDAY
SCHOOL

YOUTH
FELLOWSHIP

ATTENDERS

PUBLIC

WORK
CONTACTS

DEACONS

Dynamic	Flexible	'Who are my friends?'
Outward-looking	Bridge-building	(Matthew 12: 46-50)
Evangelizing		

Open doors
'weak'

lawyers, social workers, shop owners and managers, and approach them to offer the services of the church and enquire how Christians can begin to meet the needs of the people, as these others perceive them to be from where they are looking. The church can then enter into partnerships with others, in which these others immediately become 'stakeholders' in what the church is doing.[21]

Shortly after we first discovered this model, my wife was appointed to chair a committee in our own church, to identify appropriate ways of using our building (a large town-centre facility). She decided to adopt this approach, to see if it would work. The first person she spoke to was the manager of the shopping centre just across the road from the church. He was surprised to see her, because no one from any church had ever approached him before. But he understood well enough what was being offered, and in no time at all had produced a list of projects for the church to follow through. The agenda he came up with could have taken two or three years to work through – and other interest groups also produced their ideas of where the church's ministry might integrate with the community's needs. All in all, the opportunities that were identified could easily have represented a ten-year plan for the church. Once a church is prepared to welcome people like this as 'stakeholders' in its own organization, this relationship is quite likely to develop into a two-way stakeholding commitment, as others working to serve the community also open their structures to whatever contribution the church can make. It was no surprise to me that in due course the manager of the shopping mall invited the church to take its message into his space, in the form of singers, dancers and musicians during Advent season. It is one thing to invite others to come onto our territory to hear the Gospel: that is what we normally do, and very few come. But being ourselves invited onto other people's territory is much more important. When Jesus sent out the seventy, it was not to invite people to come to them, but themselves to be invited in (Luke 10:1–12).

Once this kind of two-way acceptance and trust takes off, the church will find itself swamped with opportunities to minister to all sorts of people within the community. But it will need to be prepared to accept people as they are, and not to bring any hidden agendas to such collaborative enterprises. The church that thinks about adopting this approach may feel intimidated at first, but be assured you will have no shortage of opportunities presented to you. The greatest restriction you are likely to find will not be the invitations coming from the community, but your own human resources and the inbred suspicion, hostility, and tunnel vision that unfortunately pervade so many of our churches.

In this approach to evangelism, ministry is not something that is delegated by the leaders to other people. It is about all of God's people sharing in the ministry of Christ wherever they are, forming partnerships with others in the community, and then inviting them to follow Jesus. And because there is no way all this can be done exclusively by clergy, the hallmark of this church will be 'a radical distribution of power to the laity. At the present the laity exists to serve the clergy's programme. The clergy will be important, but the heroes of the twenty-first century will be laity ... these, fully empowered by the church, will make the difference'.[22] Don't allow mention of the next century in that quotation to undermine the fact that this vision has ancient roots. To empower ourselves to face the future, we could do worse than look back – to places like 1 Corinthians 12, Ephesians 4:11–12, and indeed to the ministry of Jesus himself.

Open to the Spirit

If all God's people are set free to exercise ministry in the name of Christ, then by definition the church will see an explosion

of diverse ministries, for its effectiveness will no longer
depend on the gifts of only one or two people who, however
brilliant they may be, cannot be equally good at everything.
The need for the whole church to be mobilized should be obvious. Theologically, it must take the whole of the people of God
to reflect the whole of the glory of God to the world. But there
is also the simple practical consideration that unless we are
all sharing our faith then the vast majority of people will never
hear the Gospel: 'In a world where the number of people who
have no opportunity to know the story of Jesus is growing
steadily, *how necessary it is to multiply the witnessing vocation
of the church!*' [23]

Open leadership encourages both the development and the
expression of diverse gifts. It leaves room for people to be free
to be themselves. As we approach the 21st century, there will
be more people looking for more places to belong – not just
those who opt for part-time working, but also those who are in
retirement, and still want to be useful to someone. A church
that is open to accept what such people have to offer, and
actively facilitate their offerings, can expect to have no shortage of opportunity for effective evangelism.

The book of Acts specifically mentions 'prophecy and
teaching' in the church at Antioch (Acts 13:1). But no doubt
other gifts of the Spirit were also being used there. Some
believe that when Paul described the ideal Church in 1
Corinthians 12, he was looking back to what he had experienced in Antioch (it certainly did not reflect what he had
learned from Corinth!). The two ministries mentioned here by
Luke – teaching and prophecy – are representative of the two
major aspects of charismatic endowments as we find them
described in the New Testament. Teaching emphasizes the

importance of the rational understanding and presentation of the faith. This was something that Barnabas and Paul evidently specialized in, for they had spent a whole year teaching the church in Antioch (Acts 11:26). We have generally emphasized teaching to the exclusion of almost everything else, particularly in the Reformed tradition, but also more widely. We should not lose sight of the importance of thinking about our faith by allowing ourselves to be stampeded into irrationalism by the general move in that direction within western culture. We do, however, need to give urgent attention to the most appropriate ways of facilitating useful learning among Christ's followers, and that might involve the sacrifice of a few of our sacred cows. But we must not spend so much time and effort on the rational side of faith that we ignore other dimensions that are of equal importance. The church in Antioch gave teaching an honoured place, but it was also open to the non-rational and the supernatural, exemplified by the mention here of 'prophecy', which is no doubt singled out as just one example of the kind of numinous or mystical gifts that were important in the life of this church. Both aspects of ministry are important for evangelism. Teaching can (if we are lucky) change the way we think. Only the experience of spiritual power can change the way we are. Several recent writers have noted that this is what today's spiritual searchers are looking for. Jacob Needleman (himself not a Christian), complains that Christianity has become 'only a matter of words, exhortations and philosophy rather than a matter of *practical guidance* for experiencing directly the truth of the teachings', and pleads for 'the Christianity that works, that actually produces real change in human nature, real transformation'.[24] We need to be ready to face that sort of challenge.

The church in Antioch was not afraid of real transformation. They expected something to happen, and so they were not surprised when, as they were 'worshipping and fasting', God spoke (Acts 13:2). When people worship, something happens: worship really is a verb, after all! The one thing most of us need more than any other is to have a renewed awareness of the Spirit of God at work in our midst. So often, church life is routine and commonplace, and we are content for it to be so. It is worth observing, though, what happens when the church is truly open to the Spirit. The work of the Spirit among these people in Antioch certainly made a difference to their own life and witness. But it did not inspire them to think only of themselves, still less to become mere specialists in personal devotions. In Acts 11:27–30 we see how spiritual renewal led directly to social concern, as the church sent Barnabas and Paul to take practical assistance to the church in Jerusalem, which was having a hard time as a result of famine. And in Acts 13:2, attentiveness to what the Spirit was saying led to a move forward in evangelization whose repercussions were to be worldwide. This kind of church is not inward-looking, but outward-looking. The Christians of Antioch found themselves fired with a new vision for the needs of the world, and filled with a new power to meet them – and both stemmed from their sensitivity to the work of the Spirit.

Open for Mission

'God works in mysterious ways' say the words of an old hymn, and that just about sums up what happened next in Antioch. Saul and Barnabas were their very best workers. The idea that they might be sent out somewhere else must have seemed crazy, even if it was the order of an inspired prophet (Acts 13:2–3). But the obedience of the Church to that injunction was the start of the wider mission work of Paul, arguably the most successful evangelistic outreach there has ever been. As Paul's work proceeded, he sought to establish Churches along the lines of the one he knew best back in Antioch. In particular, he always trusted his converts, allowed for their natural diversity in both temperament and outlook, and as a result established a whole network of churches with mission at their centre. As far as evangelism is concerned, one of the most important books ever written on Paul was Roland Allen's slim volume *Missionary Methods – St Paul's or Ours?*[25]. He spent part of his life as a missionary in China, though his thinking was largely ignored until he was long dead, perhaps because he came from the Anglo-Catholic tradition and as a consequence was held in suspicion by the conservative evangelicals who did most to foster evangelism in the middle years of the 20th century. But he has come into his own more recently, not least because of the way he anchors his observations into solid exegesis of Paul's own letters and the book of Acts. His work is challenging to our present denominational structures, but as Lesslie Newbigin observes in the foreword to a recent reissue of his book, 'Quietly but insistently it has continued to challenge the accepted assumptions of churches and missions, and slowly but steadily the number of those who found themselves compelled to listen has increased ... this quiet voice has a strange relevance and immediacy to the problems of the Church in our day'.[26]

What was Allen saying that is so revolutionary? His understanding of Paul's method centres round five main features.

First of all, Paul refused to transplant the law and customs of
the Judean church into the Roman provinces where he
worked. In other words, he knew that the Gospel must be
translated into the culture of different peoples. But as a result,
he was often persecuted, especially by the Jews. Secondly, he
refused to set up a central administration. At the time, the
Jerusalem church was probably trying to establish itself as the
headquarters of the international Christian movement.[27] Paul
resisted that: there is only one mention in any of our sources
of a time when he acceded to the wishes of the Jerusalem
leaders, and on that occasion the narrative makes clear that he
only went along with it at the request of other people (Acts
15:1–35). Paul knew well enough that his converts needed to
be trusted and given responsibility for their own faith if they
were to be useful evangelists.

Allowing others to take responsibility for themselves is a
thread running through the other characteristics Allen identified. He notes that Paul declined to establish tests for orthodoxy. He was much happier to deal with cases of deviance as
they arose rather than laying down rules in advance. He
resisted the temptation to predict what *might* happen, preferring to act on what *did* happen. That way, he left himself space
to be able to learn even from those with whom he disagreed.
He also did not insist on every church being the same. If an
issue arose and was dealt with, Paul did not then apply the
judgement to all the other churches. The diversity of church
styles in the first century was staggering compared with the
conformity in the modern Church, where one congregation can
look pretty much the same as any other, even of a different
tradition.[28] But that was what gave the Gospel its universal
appeal. Finally, Paul encouraged churches to deal with mat-

ters of discipline corporately, instead of delegating decisions to leaders. First Corinthians 5:1–13 is perhaps the most striking example of this, where Paul (in an injunction clearly addressed to the whole congregation, not just to leaders) offers advice about dealing with a man who was cohabiting with his step-mother.

A PLACE TO BELONG

What does all this amount to? To put it simply, people need to belong. It is a basic human need.[29] If a church cannot fulfil the relational needs of its own members, then it will not be an evangelizing church. A church that tries to fit people into slots in its own pre-determined structures, rather than making space for people to exercise their own gifts and talents, will not grow. If the need to belong is not fulfilled, then those who are already in the church are likely to withdraw, lose their sense of purpose and commitment, maybe even become resentful, cynical and critical of others. It sounds too easy to say that the church should be people-centred rather than programme-centred. But it needs to be said, for a church that finds difficulty creating space for people will find it hard to leave space for God. Without space for both people and God, we are unlikely to commend the Gospel to others. In a sermon preached on 4 February 1968 in Ebenezer Baptist Church, Atlanta, Martin Luther King eloquently described the kind of church that will be evangelizing in today's world: '... the church is the one place where a doctor ought to forget he's a doctor. The church is the one place where a PhD ought to forget that he's a PhD. The church is the one place that a school-

teacher ought to forget the degree she has behind her name.
The church is the one place where the lawyer ought to forget
that he's a lawyer. And any church that violates the "whosoev-
er will, let him come" doctrine is a dead, cold church, and
nothing but a little social club with a thin veneer of religiosity.
... It's the one place where everybody should be the same
standing before a common master and saviour. And a recognition grows out of this – that all men are brothers because they
are children of a common father'. That kind of church could
easily commend the Gospel to today's spiritual searchers.

| **Putting it into Practice**

Dumbfounded! That was how I felt as I drove back home
through the cold air of a December night. Skirting the edge of
the Scottish highlands, it was not the sort of road on which you
can drive very fast at any time. In mid-winter, there was a
good chance of ice – and perhaps even a hungry stag looking
for supper on the grassy verge. So I had plenty of time for
thinking, even though the journey was little more than twenty
miles – and there was no doubt my mind was working over-
time. I had been to a party! The sort of party that, until it's
over, you never really know whether you want to go to. In some
ways, it was a pretty quiet affair. Nine or ten couples, some
married, some living together unmarried, along with a few single people. When we arrived, most of us had never met before,
so we had some introductions to make. In typical western
fashion we all described ourselves by reference to our work.
We were a very mixed bunch, with wide-ranging expertise: an
electrician, a surgeon, a forester, a bureaucrat, an engineer,
social worker, teacher, personnel adviser, car mechanic – and
more besides. Then there was me.

I remember agonizing over the most appropriate way to
introduce myself in this situation. 'Remember, this is a party',
I kept telling myself, 'these people have come here to enjoy

themselves. You'd better not come over too strong on religion.'
And so when it came to my turn I restricted my self-introduc-
tion to saying that I worked in a university. I don't mind
admitting I was deliberately trying to be as vague as possible
– and even at that one or two looked as if they might already
have been turned off by the prospect of spending an evening
with some ivory-tower academic whose knowledge was probably limited to all the things that nobody else had ever wanted
to know about. But others were curious. Was I perhaps a wizard with computers? Or some kind of scientist or technologist
pushing forward the frontiers of human knowledge? So the
inevitable supplementary soon followed: 'And which depart-
ment do you work in?' Now I knew from experience that this
could be tricky, so I opted for a fairly general reply ('religion'),
and muttered it as fast as possible, hoping that not too many
would hear. That alone can usually be guaranteed to create a
slight hiatus in the conversation – and so it did. But having
got this far, why turn back? Especially if you're curious to
know whatever could possibly attract an apparently normal
person to spend their life thinking about such a subject. In
any case, it needn't be all boring: perhaps I was an expert in
Islam, or Zen, or some other esoteric subject that would be
good for at least a couple of minutes' worth of polite conversation at a Christmas party. And, who knows, it might even be
interesting. So someone piped up, 'I suppose that will be com-
parative religion, then?'

I had a good idea what would happen next. For the true
answer to that question can go down like a lead balloon in
some circles: 'Well no. Actually I'm interested in Christianity,
and the Bible.' Sure enough, there was an audible gasp from
someone, followed by a general horrified silence. For what felt

to me like an eternity – but cannot have been longer than about two seconds – no one spoke. The floor and the ceiling suddenly became subjects of compelling fascination! But not for long. What I had said was like letting a genie out of a bottle. Soon, everyone was talking – to each other, but especially to me. 'Do you believe in God?' the hostess asked me (a particularly apposite question for a theology professor, I thought). Then 'How can a book as ancient as the Bible still make sense today?' 'What do you think happens when people pray?' 'What happens when people die?' 'Do you think Jesus was an extraterrestrial?' 'How about the prophets – were they spirit mediums, channelling in messages from some other world?' And so it went on. I can't remember whether anyone else got the chance to introduce themselves! Even when the group subsequently split up into smaller circles, those who attached themselves to me still wanted to talk about religion – and they did, until the early hours of the next morning, covering everything from the origins of evil to the power of spiritual healing, and touching all points in between. I know for certain that I and my partner were the only ones who would have qualified as 'Christians' by any definition of that word. Yet everyone else clearly believed in God. They were all educated and intelligent people (a very broad cross-section of our culture, I would say) and they were fascinated by the spiritual and supernatural. And despite the fact that none of them could see much relevance in the Church as they knew and experienced it, they all had an obvious fascination for the Bible, and its central figure, Jesus Christ.

There are millions of people like that today all over the western world. The fact is that allegedly 'secular' people are far more religious than for many generations. Twenty years ago, being religious was often regarded as a sign of weakness, or even psychological deficiency. Now, it's almost avant-garde to be engaged in the spiritual search. That search that might easily encompass all manner of seemingly bizarre and incredible beliefs and practices, but it is unlikely to have a place for whatever the Church has to offer. On hearing my opinion about the things they were interested in, some of the party-goers actually said to me, 'If you believe all this, what are you doing in the Church?' These people were not spiritually uncommitted – far from it. But what goes on in the four walls of church buildings Sunday by Sunday just made no sense to them. Even if they had been vaguely interested, they might have had a hard time just making contact with the church.

I had a salutary experience of that myself. The occasion was a student mission in a university in the north of England. I was to speak at the opening meeting on a Saturday evening, and then in a local church the following morning. My student hosts did their best to entertain me in style, but by 6 am the next morning I was awake, alone and freezing (this particular student residence had been a medieval castle, and in the meantime not much had changed). With little to detain me over breakfast, I had some time to kill before I needed to be at the church, which was a ten-minute walk from where I was staying. An even shorter walk, however, took me to the cathedral which was a major focal point of this particular city: a grand and ancient building, which I decided to explore. Being all alone in a medieval cathedral early on Sunday morning was an interesting experience. With freedom to wander, I explored all the nooks and crannies that, had there been more visitors, I would probably not have entered. Then I became aware that I was not entirely alone. I was being followed. I could hear footsteps behind me, but since their owner was not yet in sight I played games with him by running as fast as I could round different corners in the cloisters. He knew the short-cuts better than I, and eventually we met face to face. 'I'm sorry,' he said, 'but I'll have to ask you to leave.' Thinking that my little game of hide and seek had upset him, I prepared to apologize. But that was not the problem. 'They're going to have a service,' he explained, 'and it won't interest the likes of you.' With that, I was unceremoniously bundled out of a side door so that 'they' could come through the main entrance. As I made my way to the other church where I was to be the preacher, I wondered what could possibly have given this man the impression that I would not be interested in Christian faith. I concluded it could have been the way I was dressed (jeans and a leather jacket). That itself would say something. But when I related this to my family, they agreed that it was probably just an unfortunate one-off experience. More recently, I found myself with all my family in the same city, with time to spare (on this occasion it was early evening), and guess where they suggested we go? And guess what took place at the cathedral door? You've probably got it in one: all six of us were shown the way to the car park, with these words ringing in our ears, 'I'm sorry, but they're about to have a service.' Few churches would bundle people out in this officious way (though there may be more of them than I think). But our body language can easily communicate the same message. If people think they will get the brush-off from us, they are unlikely to make the effort, no matter how serious their spiritual search might be.

LEARNING FROM JESUS

What is the appropriate way to respond to the spiritual seekers of our generation? I believe the answer to that question
will be found in a fresh appreciation of how Jesus ministered.
We usually read the gospels looking for answers to questions
of a historical, literary, or theological nature. But they are not
the only possible questions, nor are they necessarily the most
useful ones in terms of evangelization. How about asking what
was actually going on in the gospels? What was Jesus looking
for? How did he relate to the people he met? And what did he
intend to happen? Asking questions like that might easily
unearth some useful guidelines for faith-sharing today. There
are any number of stories we could home in on, but there are
two passages which are particularly illuminating. These are
the story of the woman at the well (John 4:1–42) and the story
of the couple on the road to Emmaus (Luke 24:13–35). It will
be worthwhile to spend some time on them. In some ways,
they are contrasting stories. Most obviously, they come from
different gospel traditions. But for that very reason, what they
have in common is more interesting than their differences.

In Luke 24, Jesus met a married couple who were similar to
many people today. They were certainly not card-carrying,
committed disciples: if they had been they would have been
back in Jerusalem with the others, not on the road back home.
They were, in a sense, on the fringes of the church. Yet they
had not given up on belief. Quite the reverse, for their conversation revealed that they were searching for meaning in life,
and they would even like to believe in Jesus. But somehow it
had not come together for them, which is why they were heading away from the uncertainty and insecurity of Jerusalem

(where the real action was) back to the safety of their own home. Do you recognize them? Are they 'nominal' Christians, I wonder? The woman in John 4 was in a different category. She shared some of the same questions, but her situation was further complicated by what we might call an esoteric spirituality, not to mention personal moral breakdown of the sort that might well have alienated her from people like the couple in Emmaus.

Jesus bumped into both these people only once, and neither meeting took place in particularly promising circumstances. Yet in the course of these short encounters, they recognized their need of God, they began to understand who Jesus was – and then went off to share the good news with their friends. No one ever meets Jesus and stays the same. What can we learn from this? What was Jesus' secret?

Getting Alongside People

Putting it simply, Jesus was there, where these people actually were. It seems almost too obvious to say, but Jesus would never have met these people had he not been by the well and on the roadside. He was a partner in their world, and was sufficiently at home in his own culture to be able to meet people on their own territory. Clergy in particular are not supposed to hang about at wells or on roadsides. At least, that's what we would tell ourselves today. They should be in church to serve God. Of course, in a church where all the members are mobilized for faith-sharing, even that would hardly be a problem. But we often give the impression that to share faith effectively, all Christians really need to be in church buildings. So far as evangelism is concerned, modern churches generally prefer to play all their games at home, by inviting others to join us on territory where we feel safe, rather than making ourselves vulnerable by getting alongside them where they are. No matter how 'seeker-friendly' we try to make services in church, it will never be the same thing as sharing the good news on other people's territory. Even if we hire a cinema or a sports stadium that is not necessarily going to be the same thing as being alongside other people. It is all too easy to turn the cinema or stadium into a church for that occasion, and the Christians will still be in control. Just being where other people are can be painful: it might take us into places we would not normally venture. It will always be challenging. Do you remember the betting shop story in chapter 2? But if we believe that God is at work out there, then we can be confident that evangelistically productive things will take place. Knowing that God is at work in the world should empower us for witness. Jesus calls us to evangelize in the world, sharing the good news on other people's terms, in territory where we are vulnerable, and willingly so. Jesus is our model: to follow him, we are going to have to take all this more seriously than we typically do.

Affirming People's Value

Notice Jesus' opening remarks in both these episodes. At the well, he says to the woman, 'I see you have some water. I'm desperately thirsty: would you be willing to share your water with me?' Right from the start, the woman knew this was going to be something different. For a start, here was a rabbi who had needs. More than that, they were needs that he thought she could meet – and unlike other men in her life, he was not looking for sex. He accepted there was something good and positive about this woman, while also expressing his own weakness and making himself vulnerable. She could easily have told him to get lost, but already she was feeling good about herself. Here was a man who was able to listen as well as to speak.

That's exactly what Jesus did with the couple on the Emmaus road too. He walked alongside them listening to their questions. There are plenty of talkers around today. Our ears are bombarded on all sides by people with a product to market. If the only thing Christians can do is to join this cacophony, not many people will hear their message. We need to learn that sharing our faith can often begin with saying nothing at all. Dietrich Bonhoeffer expressed it so well:

Christians, especially ministers, so often think they must always contribute something when they are in the company of others, that this is the one service they have to render. They forget that listening can be a greater service than speaking. Many people are looking for an ear that will listen. They do not find it among Christians, because those Christians are talking where they should be listening. But he who can no longer listen to his brother will soon be no longer listening to God either ... One who cannot listen long and patiently will presently be talking beside the point and be never really speaking to others, albeit he is not conscious of it. Anyone who thinks that his time is too valuable to spend keeping quiet will eventually have no time for God or his brother but only for himself and for his own follies.[1]

Now think of all this in relation to so much of what passes for evangelism. I remember once asking a group of students to draw an impression of what came into their minds when they heard the word 'evangelist'. They were of different religious persuasions themselves, and their cartoons reflected that diversity. Paid-up members of the Christian Union typically drew ministers standing in pulpits preaching sermons. Other slightly more adventurous souls drew ministers standing on soap boxes at street corners, but still preaching sermons. There was only one truly creative sketch among them, and that was a full-colour depiction of Rambo. The person who drew it explained that this had been his experience of evangelists: people with rapid-fire religious guns, loaded with slick questions and answers with which to shoot down the opposition. Certainly, people who only knew how to communicate in one direction, and whose body language, let alone their words, conveyed just one message: 'You listen to what I have to say, and then decide what to do about it.'

Society is littered with the broken lives of those who have been the victims of this kind of processing. Wounded people lie all around us, crushed by those who are self-assured, assertive and directive. If Christians can only offer more of the same, why should we expect anyone to listen to us – still less to take us seriously? Remember, 'the medium is the message'. A lot of modern evangelism starts by putting people down. I have already suggested this happens because we have a shallow view of sin. As a result, there is little compassion in our evangelism, and hurting people head off elsewhere to find value and acceptance.

The Gospel, however, always lifts people up.[2] Faced with the woman at the well, Jesus affirmed her and recognized her value as a person. Can you imagine the field-day some of today's moralistic busy-bodies might have had with a woman with her lifestyle? Jesus could see well enough that she was a sinner, but he had no need to tell her because she knew that only too well herself. He did, however, see her as someone who had been seriously sinned-against, and had compassion on her – and that certainly marked him out as different. Many of those to whom we are called to witness are in the same predicament, and saying, as Jesus did, 'You are a person of value' can easily lead to a great evangelistic harvest.

A Christian worker was walking round a public housing estate one Sunday afternoon. The rain was lashing down, and a gale was blowing. There seemed little possibility for faith-sharing here. The only sign of life was someone up a ladder trying to repair a leaking gutter. As he walked nearer, the Christian could see that the person up the ladder was a girl about seven years old. The rain was cascading like a waterfall over the door, inside which a drunk man was sheltering, shouting instructions to the child on the ladder. It turned out that he wanted to go to the bar for another drink, but needed the gutter fixed so he could leave home without getting soaked through. The evangelist (for that is what he was) summed up the situation, and decided to help the girl. He went up the ladder, and fixed the gutter. The girl was delighted: she was saved from her precarious perch. So was her father: he got his drink. The evangelist had mixed feelings. What could such an action possibly have to do with sharing the Gospel? About two weeks later, he got the answer to his question. The man and the girl – and other members of the same family – turned up out of the blue at the church. For somebody to care that much for a little girl whose father was in a drunken stupor had spoken powerfully to them. The father knew he had done wrong: he needed no one to tell him. If the evangelist had told him so on that wet afternoon, he would probably have cursed and sent him packing. As it was, the family came to faith. That incident happened in Scotland, but similar things are happening around the world when Christians see others as sinned-against and, like Jesus, have compassion on them.[3] We have too many evangelists like Rambo, and too few like Jesus.

Addressing People's Needs

We took a lot of space in a previous chapter reflecting on how important it is to address people at their point of need. It makes no sense to repeat it here. But it is worth reading these stories carefully to see how Jesus went about addressing personal needs. The Emmaus couple had a problem with the Old Testament because they could not reconcile what they understood of its teaching with what had happened on the cross. Jesus joined them in their discussion, and using the methodology we highlighted in chapter 2, he helped them to address their questions to the text, moving them on in their reflections, and giving them an opportunity to learn from their experiences. We are unlikely to meet too many people with questions about the Old Testament – or, for that matter, the New Testament. Of course, we feel happiest talking about such topics, which is why we are tempted to do it all the time. But if we insist on setting our own agenda, we ought not to be surprised if no one else is interested. Jesus followed an adaptive strategy. He was not primarily message-centred, but people-centred. The message was not expressed in the same terms for everyone. Jesus knew he would only connect with others if the message was relevant for each person and situation.

Martin Luther observed that people are 'captivated more readily by comparisons and examples than by difficult and subtle disputations. They would rather see a well-drawn picture than a well-written book.'[4] People today still discover faith this way. I must have preached thousands of sermons in the last twenty years, many of them very good sermons. But sermons rarely have the same power as pictures to challenge and change people's lives. My wife has a specialist Christian ministry in the creative arts, particularly clowning, and particularly in worship (which, you will recall, is an essential part of authentic evangelization). I remember an occasion when she joined a dance group who were working with the song 'Shine, Jesus, Shine'. Attracted by the colour and the music, Valentine the clown came in, hesitantly at first, and was gradually drawn into the movement, ultimately transformed as she knelt at the foot of the cross. A social worker said afterwards, 'That was me at the foot of that cross'. Or another occasion in Perth, Western Australia, where the crosses over Valentine's eyes were used to spell out the message that for true transformation we need to look at the world the way God sees it – through the cross – and a teenage boy who was there found his concerns about the environment, peace, justice and violence, picked up in such a way that he too was drawn closer to Christ. I can think of a workshop on spirituality in southern California, where people were moving in a circle dance to the song by Scots musician Ian White, 'Praise the Lord, all you servants of the Lord' (Psalm 134). In the circle, we put our hands palm to palm with the people next to us, and raised them to form a giant crown in praise of God the sovereign – and that action alone brought healing and freedom into the life of more than one person who had previously been sexually abused. I could go on. People's needs are all different. Jesus calls us to recognize them, and then to address them in appropriate ways – and that will not always mean in words. Remember that other text about loving the Lord with the heart, soul and strength, as well as the mind.

Waiting for People to Join Us

Jesus always gave people space to work out how to respond to him. Take the couple at Emmaus. He had moved them on in their understanding, and when he got to the door of their home he gave them the chance to go on – in a direction of their choosing. They had the freedom either to leave the encounter, or to invite him to join them. Jesus did not pressurize them, or force them into a corner. He recognized their freedom as persons, and the couple chose to invite him in.

At Emmaus Jesus had no need to create a space. It was already there, as the trio arrived at the front door: the natural dynamic of the situation meant a choice had to be made. Jesus respected that, and did not invite himself. The opposite, in fact, for Luke says 'he walked ahead as if he were going on' (Luke 24:28). With the woman at the well, Jesus needed to create a space. In this instance, he did it by suggesting she went to get her husband. As soon as he said that, she knew she had the opportunity to make choices. No doubt Jesus could have criticized her marital arrangements. To do so would have been incompatible with the way he had already affirmed her as a person. It is worth noting that Jesus' approach, valuing her and addressing her need, did not lead (as some might imagine) to a woolly Gospel. It actually put

Jesus in a uniquely credible position from which to challenge her. True evangelism always starts where people are, but then opens up opportunities for them to move closer to God.

In Luke 15, Jesus told three parables about lost things. It is instructive to observe how those lost things were found.[5] In two cases (the sheep, vv 4–7, and the coin, vv 8–10), their owners took an active role and went out to find them. But in the third case (vv 11–31), the father did not follow his lost son into the far country, nor go looking for him in the pig sty. He stayed at home, and waited for his return. Expectantly waiting, of course, prayerfully waiting no doubt – but waiting all the same. There is nothing contradictory between these two dynamics of evangelization. Sometimes activism is appropriate. It is certainly an easier posture than waiting, for it enables us to think we are doing something, and we all like to feel busy. But waiting will always have a key role in effective evangelism. no one was ever intimidated into God's Kingdom. 'True witness follows Jesus Christ in respecting and affirming the uniqueness and freedom of others. .... The Spirit of God is constantly at work in ways that pass human understanding and in places that to us are least expected ...'[6]

LEARNING BY DOING

Several years ago, I found myself sitting in a plane next to an obviously rich and successful businessman. Not quite next to him, for it was a row of three seats and between the two of us was an empty place. Its message was pretty clear: we were not meant to speak to each other. Nor did we for some considerable time. Not until the flight attendant arrived with a drink, and as a tray was passed along the row our eyes met for an instant. It was enough to break the ice, and we began a tentative conversation. As we talked, this man confided in me that he had problems. That very morning he had slammed the door of his home for the last time. His marriage was under stress. His growing children were giving cause for concern. And he was personally unfulfilled. The only thing to do was to leave them to get on with it, and try to find satisfaction alone somewhere else.

I was actually on my way to a conference on evangelism where I was scheduled to give one of the keynote addresses. I knew there was no way I could deliver that address with integrity if I did not share my faith in Christ with this person. But how? Frankly, I had no idea. So I did what most of us do when we are in a real fix: I prayed. A silent, momentary prayer that God would give me the words to say. Before I had time to think about it I found myself asking a question. 'Do you know God?', I said to the person alongside me. At that very instant my whole life seemed to flash before my eyes – like the last moments of a drowning man. What a stupid thing to say, I thought to myself. Why had I not said something more conventional? Like, 'Have you been to church lately?' Or, 'Have you thought of consulting a priest?' Even, perhaps, 'Have you read the Bible?' Or whatever. But it was too late for second thoughts: I had already asked my question.

If the question surprised me, the answer bowled me over completely. 'As a matter of fact, I don't,' my companion replied, 'but if you know something about God, I'd like to know more.' At the end of the flight, I gave him my address and we went our separate ways. Two or three weeks later I had a letter from this same person. In it, he told me how at his destination he had been unable to get our conversation out of his mind. He saw a church with an open door, went in, and there he prayed as best he knew how that God would somehow intervene directly in his life. In due course, his business was completed and he had to face going home again. For all his bravado, he had nowhere else to stay. In any case, he thought that would be a real test for God. When he finally returned, he was surprised to receive a warm welcome from his wife. Even more surprised to hear what she had to say. The morning he left home, she too had felt it was all over. As she left her children at the school gate, she shared her feelings with another parent. The other person was planning to go to a prayer group that very day. It wasn't meant to be an evangelistic group, but how could an obvious need like this be ignored? So the two of them went together. The woman was immediately attracted by the warmth of the group. In fact, the group prayed for the husband on the plane – at exactly the moment that I was in conversation with him. As a direct result, it seemed, both husband and wife had met God in a new and challenging way that subsequently transformed their marriage, their family and their entire outlook on life. For my part, I was surprised to discover that my companion was not only a successful businessman: he was the chief executive of the airline. And the seat between us was empty because he had booked it to make sure no one spoke to him!

I have often reflected on that encounter, and tried to analyse exactly what happened. What did I do? Well, I gave the man space to speak or not as he might choose. Then I listened to what he had to say, for a considerable time as it turned out. And I asked one question! Without realizing it, I had followed exactly the strategy of Jesus. It was a year or two later that it dawned on me how Jesus communicated. He listened to people, he asked questions and he told stories. And, of course, he lifted people up. That might be more difficult.

There are two things most of us definitely don't know how to do. We don't know how to affirm and stand alongside others without somehow compromising ourselves. And we don't know how to challenge people. Jesus had this marvellous facility for just being available to people, and then almost casually digging them in the ribs and saying, 'Oh, by the way, do you fancy being my disciple?' We have something to learn from him on all this. Because it's not a programme we have to buy into, sharing faith this way will not require costly investment from limited church budgets. Nor will we need to import experts to evangelize for us: every Christian, no matter who they are, can work this way. The weaker we are, the more successful we are likely to be. Once we grasp that we have something to share with others not because we are different from them, but precisely because we are no different – well, that will be really good news, for us as well as for those we are called to evangelize.

appendix one | Conversion and Faith-Development

In discussing the nature of conversion in chapter 4, reference was briefly made to the work of various Christian educators, and the possibility of relating the faith journey to the life cycle, particularly by utilizing insights from developmental psychology that might help to explain how and why faith seems to take on different forms at different stages of life.

The idea that the life of faith passes through various stages is nothing new. In their book *The Critical Journey*, Janet Hagberg and Robert Guelich trace it back into the early Christian centuries, and identify an impressive array of people whose experience of faith seems to have been like this: Augustine, Julian of Norwich, Teresa of Avila, Francis of Assisi, Ignatius – and then, into modern times, with Sören Kierkegaard, Evelyn Underhill, Scott Peck, and others. 'It soon becomes apparent that, if not agreement, at least some parallels exist in the description of the direction by many writers/faith seekers on the journey of faith.'

In biblical terms, the idea that faith is a journey rather than a single ecstatic episode in a person's life goes right back into the Old Testament, where the journey motif is all-pervasive, and being nurtured as part of the community of faith is central to personal faith-commitment. The same emphasis comes through in many parts of the New Testament, where it is stressed that following Jesus is more than just making a single choice: it also involves learning, being built up in faith, and, indeed, ultimately becoming like Christ.[2] That all makes sense in the light of the passages we have studied previously, for if conversion is more than just an instantaneous episode, then it must potentially be a lifelong process: 'Christianity must touch all areas of a person's life: thinking, feeling, and doing'.[3]

But how does the faith journey work? James Fowler has been a pioneer in this field. In the ideas of developmental psychologists Erikson, Piaget and Kohlberg, he found a useful framework within which to express a concept of 'stages of faith'.[4] The six stages of faith that Fowler identified are listed on the diagram, along with Erikson's eight ages of man for comparison. In recent years, these notions have given rise to widespread debate, and Fowler has continually revised his model, though always within the six-stage framework.[5]

'Faith' itself is one concept that has generated much discussion. Fowler (adopting the ideas of one of his own teachers, Wilfred Cantwell Smith) assumed that 'faith' is something everyone has, and it is not the same thing as believing in religious systems and structures, but is the basic way in which we all make sense out of things.[6] On this understanding, 'faith' becomes something like 'worldview', as long as we think of that not in propositional but in personal terms as 'the stories I use to make sense out of it all'. This opinion has much to commend it inasmuch as it reminds us that faith can be a verb as well as a noun,[7] and in the context of evangelism it helps us understand why, for instance, Paul could use the (mistaken) views of the Athenians as pegs on which to hang the Gospel, or why Jesus, instead of getting involved in complex debates about theology contented himself with pointing to a different (and better) way of seeing things than his questioners had.[8]

Inevitably there are many detailed questions that could be addressed to this kind of scheme. If we think of it as a rigid structure into which everyone's experience of God must be made to fit, then it will be less than useful. In reality, these stages of faith are rather like stills taken from a particular movie. They are not therefore normative for what should be in every other movie. They describe what faith is, and how it develops, but they do not prescribe what faith must be for every person. Much of the criticism of Fowler has centred around this point, in particular the view that his stages are based on a male (even macho) way of understanding human development.[9] They certainly need to be broadened out to include more of the emotional side of human experience.[10]

Fowler has demonstrated that life, and faith, develop hand-in-hand, and to try to address the one without taking account of the other is likely to be a futile undertaking. Even Neill Q. Hamilton, who is critical of any attempt to link psychological development with Christian faith, still insists that life is about change, and evangelism must therefore relate to that.[11]

One of the most promising expositions of all this is in the work of Janet Hagberg and Robert Guelich, not least because they have been prepared to use their own personal faith stories to illustrate their work. They have been able to pick up many of the criticisms of Fowler's early work, and eliminate some of his weaknesses while building on his strengths. They place themselves firmly in the mainstream of the Protestant theological tradition, and take both theology and the Bible seriously. Their description of stages corresponds very closely

Stages of Life and Faith Development

Eric Erickson Eight Ages of man	James Fowler Stages of Faith	Janet Hagberg and Robert Guelich The Critical Journey	Peter New Testament
1 BASIC TRUST Infancy: "Somebody is there and somebody loves me"	**1 INTUITIVE/PROJECTIVE** "God is like my mum and dad" Discovery through relationships	**Influenced by External Sources and Stimuli:** **1 THE RECOGNITION OF GOD** "Who is God? Who am I?"	**1 "I BELIEVE IN GOD"** Personal and spiritual growth within Judaism
2 ACHIEVING AUTONOMY Age 2 - 3: "Let me do it"	**2 MYTHICAL-LITERAL** "What's fair is fair" getting things into order	**2 THE LIFE OF DISCIPLESHIP** Sense of belonging/group identification	**2 "JESUS SEEMS A GOOD GUY"** Adoption of a role model/a place to belong (Mark 1)
3 EXPANDING IMAGINATION Age 4 - 6: "I am what I can imagine I will be"	**3 SYNTHETIC CONVENTIONAL** "I believe what the church believes" Conforming to other people's expectations	**3 THE PRODUCTIVE LIFE** "Giving to and for others - within limits "	**3 "I NEED TO THINK THIS OUT"** Jesus is the Messiah! (Mark 8)
4 A SENSE OF INDUSTRY Age 6 -12: "I really can do it " – learning and making	**4 INDIVIDUATIVE/REFLECTIVE** "As I see it God is …." Thinking things through	**Centred Around Self-Discovery and Transformation:** **4 THE JOURNEY INWARD** Re-evaluation of faith and life: "What am I worth, and to whom?"	**4 "CAN I REALLY LOVE HIM THIS MUCH?"** (John 18, 21)
5 IDENTITY Adolescence: "Who am I ?"	**5 CONJUNCTIVE** "Distinguishing the map from the territory " Seeing a broader picture, especially in relation to emotions	**The Wall'** **5 THE JOURNEY OUTWARD** "Living with uncertainty "	**5 "WHO IS GOD, WHO AM I, WHAT AM I ABOUT?"** (Acts 10/Gal. 2:11-14)
6 INTIMACY Young adult: need to belong, participate	**6 UNIVERSALIZING** "I have a dream" The big vision	**6 THE LIFE OF LOVE** Loving God, self, others	**6 "SHARING MYSELF AND MY FAITH"** Galilee, Antioch, Rome, 1 Peter etc.
7 GENERATIVITY 30s-60s: making, producing – achievements, family, etc			
8 FACING DEATH "It has all been worthwhile "			

to Fowler's, as the diagram shows. But they adopt a more flexible approach, describing their work as 'a loose guide, a globe rather than a road map'.[12] For them, movement within the life of faith revolves around two pivotal points: God's actions in a person's life, and the personal response itself. This corresponds quite closely to what we identified in the life of Peter, where faith seems to be about making active choices, and letting God into different areas of life, something which can be described as 'a continual process of growth rather than a point of arrival'.[13] A two-dimensional diagram does not, however, fully reflect the dynamic nature of this model of faith development. For on this model, faith does not proceed in a linear progression from one stage to another. It is, for example, possible to get stuck in different stages, even to move back to earlier stages. The image of a coiled spring referred to in chapter 4 is a better visual aid here.

In thinking about all this in relation to evangelism, it seems to me that understanding where people are at in their faith journey will help us to communicate the Gospel in relevant ways. To help people find Christ, we need to know their starting points, otherwise how can we set up effective signposts to move them in the right direction? There will be for everyone an appropriate response to God at each stage of life and faith, and there are probably different kinds of challenge and change that will be relevant at different stages. Some try to distinguish between two different types of 'conversion' experience, and that may be a helpful way to think about it. R. Moseley, for instance, differentiates 'structural' conversion (the reorientation of basic assumptions), from 'lateral' conversion (changes in the contents of one's faith).[14] In terms of Peter's story, 'structural conversion' may be an appropriate way to describe his first encounter with Jesus, while 'lateral conversion' could approximate more closely to some of the other episodes (though what took place at the house of Cornelius looks much more like a 'structural' change). However we label things, there is wide agreement that change from one stage to another does not happen automatically, but is brought about by 'crises, novelties, and experiences of disclosure and challenge which threatens the limits of the person's present patterns of constitutive-knowing'.[15] That is what was happening on the Emmaus road and at the Samaritan well, where Jesus either created or utilized spaces in which challenges could be faced and new choices made. Indeed, one author actually traces five significant stages of faith development within the Emmaus story, which he believes can be taken as a paradigm for the total conversion experience.[16]

Placing the story of Peter alongside the other models helps to anchor all this in a particular biblical example. The various points of challenge and change which can be identified in his coming to faith actually parallel fairly clearly the stages identified by Hagberg and Guelich, and their delineation of the various stages can be correlated quite easily with the episodes in the life of Peter. Their notion that it is possible to go back a stage, as well as forward, appears over and over again in Peter's experience (most notably, perhaps, after Caesarea Philippi and again after the episode in the house of Cornelius). Hagberg and Guelich do not themselves adopt Peter as a model, preferring others from Old Testament as well as New. But in biblical terms, Peter's seems to be the most comprehensive example of the faith journey, probably because it is so well documented, though with more intensive scrutiny I believe Paul could also be used to demonstrate the same thing.

In terms of practical faith-sharing, we would of course place our own experience of faith within this matrix, as we set 'the hope that is within us' alongside the faith journeys of others to whom we witness, confident in the knowledge that since God is at work out there, something creative will happen. This then becomes another tool helping to clarify the interactive relationship between the three dynamic elements of mission outlined in chapter 3: God's story, the Bible stories, and personal stories (our own and other people's).

Faith-Sharing Today: a Personal Story

This story was shared with me by a member of a group that I was running in Berkeley, California in July 1992. It is unique, and personal to that individual. But her experience is very typical of the kind of person we will need to reach with the Gospel. It is included here to stimulate reflection, and also to give some insight into why so many spiritually sensitive people head off in the opposite direction from the Church when they really want to find God. A lot of people feel this way about the Church. As you read it, ask yourself what you would do to share the good news with a person like this.

I see much of what I have longed for in the Church in New Age therapies and practices. This has come from my own search for psychological and spiritual healing. I have been in the Church (all different types) and a Christian since a child. I'd like to give an overview of 'my story'. My sharing of the material in this group will come out of my experience and attempts to integrate it into the whole of my life.

I have known Jesus since I was a young child and have been involved in evangelical and charismatic churches (sort of a love-hate relationship) and para-church ministries all my life. My heart has been toward the more relational and experiential aspects of faith although the intellectual and rational

are important to me also. My main interest has been in facilitating the forming of small home groups for sharing, support,
prayer and whatever else seems good. I am forty-eight years
old, married, the mother of four children, two of whom are
adopted and with disabilities. I am a physical therapist but
work only occasionally part-time, as my family's needs allow. I
am a survivor of childhood emotional and sexual abuse and
the oldest child in a fragmented multi-divorce family. I have
eight younger siblings – half, step, and one whole brother who
has schizophrenia and for whom many have prayed for healing
and deliverance. I have witnessed and experienced many
supernatural spiritual phenomena.

As I have struggled to bring healing and wholeness to my
family – so I have done in the church. I thought of myself as
God's little helper, 'Jesus in me' – I always knew we could
make a difference. Outwardly I was peaceful, compassionate
and wise but inwardly I was afraid, confused, paralysed by
denied feelings of anger and shame and desperately seeking
relief from constant depression, anxiety and chronic pain. I
didn't know why I felt that way. And who would believe me if I
told them? Well, I supposed Jesus would heal me and take
care of me if I just continued to 'die to self' and be faithful to
him and to others. Yet even when I tried to reach out for help,
the doors seemed closed. After eventually hitting the wall –
spiritually, psychologically and physically – I am on a personal and desperate journey to find healing. I came to this group
as part of that journey.

On this fearful, life-or-death, journey, I am finding hope,
understanding and support – but mostly outside the 'Church'
and traditional Christian ministries. I am letting go of old
belief systems, happy endings (in this life), my old identity

and relationship with Jesus and many other things. I am getting new glimpses of the power of the cross, self-knowledge that I hope will lead me to a more true knowledge of God, more honest relationships and an amazing exposure to the 'healing arts' – some of which could be called New Age. I am thankful that at a basic level I am grounded in Christ and that I will eventually fall back into his arms. I am not afraid of the no-no's any more. I am aware of my vulnerability but confident of my discernment. I have learned so much – my world is so much bigger – God seems so much bigger. I am also overwhelmed by the pain and lostness and searching – as in my family.

I hope some day to integrate body – mind – spirit – spirit therapies/ministry in a Christian context. I have a heart for the wounded and compromised – we'll see how that develops.

Church is hard for me. It seems so patriarchal, patronizing at best, with little room for women whose gifts and calling are towards the spiritual welfare and visionary realm of the Church. Control is an issue when it comes to trying new forms and styles of worship and ministry. I still see small groups as the best way to encourage relational, personal and experiential growth. As Christians experience the 'real thing' – New Agers *will* notice.

As I am healed I hope I will be more confident in who I am and what I can give. I hope there will be a place for me – to give, to receive. This group has been and will be invaluable to me in evaluating my 'exposures' and in being more confident as I come alongside New Age philosophies, practices, and *people*.

Endnotes

Chapter 1 Faith, Culture and the 21st Century

1 J L Steffens, *Autobiography* (New York: Literary Guild, 1931), p 799.

2 Joanna Lumley, *Stare Back and Smile*, quoted in *Woman's Weekly*, 9 October 1990, p 26.

3 *TS Beat* issue 9 (1990), p 6.

4 M Ferguson, *The Aquarian Conspiracy* (London: Paladin, 1982), p 77.

5 For extensive discussion of this question, see Lesslie Newbigin, *Foolishness to the Greeks* (Geneva: WCC, 1986); *The Gospel in a Pluralist Society* (London: SPCK, 1989).

6 Cf the personal testimony of Kenneth Wapnick, the New Age author of *Forgiveness and Jesus* (Roscoe, NY: Foundation for 'A Course in Miracles', 1983), who contrasts the way that 'Christianity has been a religion of sacrifice, guilt, persecution, murder and elitism' with 'Jesus its primary symbol – he whose Gospel was only love, forgiveness, peace and unity', and goes on to observe somewhat ruefully that 'Christianity has not been very Christian' (p 9). For a more comprehensive analysis of how Christianity has failed to provide the west with a meaningful spirituality, cf also (among many others) F Capra, *The Turning Point* (New York: Simon & Schuster, 1982); J Needleman, *Lost Christianity* (Garden City, NY: Doubleday, 1980).

7 Petronius, *Satyricon* 17.

8 By contrast, there are only 30,000 Christian clergy of all types. In France 40,000 professional astrologers are registered for tax purposes, compared with 26,000 Roman Catholic priests. Cf *MARC Newsletter* 93/3 (September 1993), p 2.

9 On Hitler, cf Nicholas Goodrick-Clarke, *The Occult Roots of Nazism* (Wellingborough: Aquarian Press, 1985); for the influence of neo-paganism on Hitler, through Wagner, see M Brearley, 'Hitler & Wagner: the Leader, the Master and the Jews', in *Patterns of Prejudice* 22/2 (1988), pp 3–22.

10 R L Ackoff, *Creating the Corporate Future* (New York: John Wiley & Sons, 1981), pp 4–5. For a readable and well-informed analysis of the nature and rate of change by a Christian writer, see Russell Chandler, *Racing Toward 2001* (Grand Rapids: Zondervan, 1992).

11 S Weil, 'Some thoughts on the love of God', in R Rees (ed), *Science, Necessity, and the love of God* (London: OUP, 1968), p 148.

12 Quoted by Charles Krauthammer, 'The Greatest Cold War Myth of All', in *Time* 142/23 (29 November 1993), p 84.

13 On the western press and Islam, see N Daniel, *Islam and the West: the making of an image* (Edinburgh: Edinburgh University Press, 1960); E W Said, *Covering Islam: how the media and the experts determine how we see the rest of the world* (London: Routledge & Kegan Paul, 1985).

14 In the 1980s, an average of one new mosque opened every two weeks in Britain, a rate of growth paralleled also in France and Germany. Much of the growth of the Islamic community is due to births and immigration. But increasing numbers of western people are converting to Islam, mostly as western women marry into Muslim families, but also among people who are attracted by the moral demands Islam places on believers, and Afro-Caribbeans alienated by prevailing cultural values.

15 These and other statistics relating to the growth and decline of the Church are mostly taken from *The World Christian Encyclopedia*, edited by David B Barrett (New York: OUP, 1982), and regular updates published by him in a variety of journals.

16 According to recent projections, by the year 2000 55 per cent of all Protestant missionaries will be non-western, and the figures are similar for the Roman Catholic church. Cf J H Kraakevik and D Welliver, *Partners in the Gospel* (Wheaton: Billy Graham Center, 1992), pp 161–175.

17 For a stimulating account of all this, see Charles Handy, *The Age of Unreason* (London: Business Books, 1989).

18 See *Social Trends 1993* (London: Central Statistical Office); and *Family Lifestyles* (London: Mintel, 1993). Tom Griffin, editor of *Social Trends 1990*, observed then that 'If this trend continues, by the end of the century no baby will be born in wedlock.'

19 Peter and Sue Kaldor, *Where the River Flows* (Homebush West, NSW: Lancer, 1988), p xxiii.

20 Tom Forrest, 'An opportunity not to be lost', in *New Evangelization 2000* 13 (1990), p 8.

Chapter 2 Where do We go from Here?

1 Anyone who doubts that latter claim need only select at random any commentary on any book of the Bible written in the last couple of centuries, to discover that they all start from the assumption that we can best understand things by taking them to pieces. Theories on source documents and ultimate origins of the biblical materials all feature prominently in the basic tool-kit of today's Bible interpreter. We have convinced ourselves that, once you can discover what a piece of literature is made of, you also know what it means. You don't, of course: if you are very lucky, you might just manage to come up with some approximate idea of what it is made of. But such is our love affair with the reductionist model that very few stop to make that observation.

2 See, for example, R L Ackoff, *Creating the Corporate Future*, esp. ch. 1, pp 3–24; M Ferguson, *The Aquarian Conspiracy*, esp. ch. 11, pp 397–426; J Needleman, *Lost Christianity*.

3 Even the development of western science has sometimes relied on intuitions for significant advances. In 1865, the German chemist August Kekule had a dream in which the benzene molecule was like a snake whirling around biting its own tail. He took that picture seriously, and as a result not only described the chemical structure of benzene for the first time, but came up with a hypothesis that explained other hitherto unknown aspects of organic chemistry.

4 Shirley Maclaine, *Out on a Limb* (London: Bantam, 1983), p 215.

5 Bhagwan Shree Rajneesh, *I am the Gate* (New York: Harper & Row, 1977), p 18.

6 A good example of this is the way the western New Age takes over and reinterprets eastern concepts of reincarnation. In the east, reincarnation always has a moral basis: how a person will come back next time depends on the way they behave now. Westerners, however, have too strong a sense of their own individual importance to accept that, and so typically talk of choosing their own karma, and deciding who they will be in each life – thereby destroying and distorting the very basis of the belief they claim to be espousing. For example: cf J L Simmons, *The Emerging New Age* (Santa Fe: Bear & Co, 1990); and critical comment in my *What is the New Age saying to the Church?* (London: Marshall Pickering, 1991), pp 95–134.

7 See, for example, Shirley Maclaine, *Out on a Limb*, pp 234–235.

8 Cf K Copeland, *The Laws of Prosperity* (Fort Worth: Copeland Ministries, 1974), *Walking in the Realm of the Miraculous* (Fort Worth: Copeland Ministries, 1979). For a critical analysis, cf J A Matta, *The Born Again Jesus of the Word-Faith Teaching* (Los Osos: Spirit of Truth, 1987).

9 The rise of Liberation Theology is perhaps the most striking example of this trend, though it is not the only one. Cf P Berryman, *Liberation Theology* (London: Tauris, 1987); T Witvliet, *A Place in the Sun* (Maryknoll, NY: Orbis, 1985); Robert McAfee Brown, *Liberation Theology, an introductory guide* (Louisville: Westminster/John Knox, 1993).

10 For a succinct account of this model and its development, cf W Hankey, 'The Bible in a Post-Critical Age', in W Oddie (ed), *After the Deluge* (London: SPCK, 1987), pp 41–92.

11 That is not to say, of course, that such study has nothing to offer. By placing the story of the near-sacrifice of Isaac, for example, into its historical context it is possible to appreciate that, in the context of a patriarchal society, 'a man's children are seen as extensions of his own value and significance and are not considered as uniquely important human beings in their own right', so 'Isaac is that which Abraham values and prizes the most, effectively his most precious possession' [R W L Moberly, 'Christ as the key to Scripture: Genesis 22 Reconsidered', in R S Hess, P E Satterthwaite, G J Wenham, *He Swore an Oath* (Cambridge: Tyndale House, 1993), p 156]. But while such observations may tone down some of the text's implications for modern readers, they do not begin to address the contemporary situation, nor indeed to show how stories like this relate to the wider Christian theological tradition, not least the teaching of Jesus where children seem to be given a rather special significance (Mark 9:33–37, 42; 10:13–16).

12 For the use of masks in exegesis, worship and spirituality, see Prof. Doug Adams, 'Facing the Cain in Ourselves', in *Church Teachers* 20/2 (1992), pp 58–59.

13 Even in the original context of the Genesis story there is significance in the fact that it is God who steps in to rescue Sarah (12:17–20), Hagar/Ishmael (21:14–20), and Isaac (22:11–14).

14 For discussion of the differences between the two, cf E V McKnight, *Post-Modern Use of the Bible* (Nashville: Abingdon Press, 1988). For presentation and critical examination of more interactive ways of textual interpretation, see C Rowland and M Corner, *Liberating Exegesis* (London: SPCK, 1990); F Watson, *The Open Text* (London: SCM Press, 1993); R S Sugirtharajah (ed), *Voices from the Margin* (London: SPCK, 1991).

15 R McAfee Brown, *Liberation Theology*, pp 81–82.

16 See R McAfee Brown, *Unexpected News* (Philadelphia: Westminster Press, 1984), pp 21–32

17 L White Jr, 'The historical roots of our ecological crisis', *Science* vol 155 (10 March, 1967), pp 1203–1207.

18 For a more detailed discussion of some of these issues, cf my article 'Defining a Biblical Theology of Creation', in *Transformation* 10/2 (April/June 1993), pp 7–11; also my *The Bible, Fact or Fantasy?* (Oxford: Lion, 1989), pp 125–150.

19 Anyone who doubts the influence of this view need look no further than some of the political theorists who most inspired the development of Thatcherism in the 1980s, and emphasized exactly this point as a way of providing a religious (Christian) foundation for their socio-economic ideas. Cf M Novak, *The Spirit of Democratic Capitalism* (New York: Simon & Schuster 1982); J Davies (ed), *God and the Marketplace* (London: Institute of Economic Affairs, Health & Welfare Unit, 1993); D Anderson (ed), *The Kindness that Kills* (London: SPCK, 1984).

20 Cited in M Fox, *Original Blessing* (Santa Fe: Bear & Co, 1983), p 11.

21 Cf M Fox, *Original Blessing; Whee! We, Wee All the Way Home* (Santa Fe: Bear & Co, 1981). For a discussion of Fox's position in relation to biblical exegesis, see Andrew Deeter Dreitcer, 'A New Creation', in *The Way* 29/1 (1989), pp 4–12. In the same issue of *The Way*, Thomas E Clarke gives a useful introduction to the subject ('Creational Spirituality', pp 68–80). I am myself far from uncritical of Fox's arguments, but I believe what he says about sin and blessing is drawing our attention to some issues that are fundamental to the task of evangelization at this point in history. His other book, *The Coming of the Cosmic Christ* (San Francisco: Harper & Row, 1988) raises different kinds of questions, and promulgates what I would regard as a deviant Christology, but that should not be allowed to detract from the validity and usefulness of his other works.

22 For critiques of Fox, cf Ted Peters, *The Cosmic Self* (San Francisco: Harper, 1991), pp 120–131; Jane E Strohl, 'The Matthew Fox Phenomenon', in *Word & World* 8 (Winter 1988), pp 42–47; M Brearley, 'Matthew Fox: Creation Spirituality for the Aquarian Age', in *Christian Jewish Relations* 22/2 (1989), pp 37–49; M Perry, *Gods Within* (London: SPCK, 1992), pp 76–84; C Noble, 'Matthew Fox's Cosmic Christ – a critical response', in *Crux* (XXVII) 1991, pp 21–29.

23 John Finney, *Finding Faith Today* (Swindon: Bible Society, 1992), pp 33–34

24 *Finding Faith Today*, p 20.

25 Peter Brierley, *Christian England* (London: MARC Europe, 1991), p 148.

26 *Christian England*, p 93.

27 The title of chapter 1 in M McLuhan, *Understanding Media* (London: Routledge & Kegan Paul, 1964).

28 Quoted in M Fox, *Whee! We, Wee All the Way Home*, p 4.

29 Descartes, 'Discourse on the Method', part 4, section 32 (in J Cottingham, R Stoothoff, D Murdoch (eds), *Philosophical Writings of Descartes*, Cambridge: CUP, 1985, vol. 1, p 127).

30 Cf C Darwin, *The Experience of the emotions in Man and Animals*, originally published in 1872 (popular edition London: John Murray, 1904).

31 A Mehrabian, *Silent Messages* (Belmont, CA: Wadsworth, 1971).

32 R L Birdwhistell, *Kinesics and Context* (London: Allan Lane, 1971) discovered that the average person actually speaks words for a total of only about ten or eleven minutes a day, and the average sentence takes about 2.5 seconds. He estimated that more than 65 per cent of all communication takes place non-verbally.

33 *Christian England*, p 206.

Chapter 3 Back to the Beginning

1 On Galilee, see S de Freyne, *Galilee from Alexander the Great to Hadrian* (Wilmington: Glazier, 1980). For the view that Galilee was more sophisticated and religious than is usually supposed, see Shmuel Safrai, 'The Jewish cultural nature of Galilee in the first century', in M Lowe (ed), The New *Testament and Christian-Jewish Dialogue: studies in honor of David Flusser* (Jerusalem: Ecumenical Theological Research Fraternity, 1993, pp. 147-186.)

2 Cf J D G Dunn, 'Methodology of Evangelism in the New Testament' (an unpublished paper written for the Evangelism Committee of the British Council of Churches).

3 On the hermeneutical challenges presented by the letter form of the New Testament, see M D Hooker, *Pauline Pieces* (London: Epworth, 1979), pp 7-20; C J Roetzel, *The Letters of Paul* (London: SCM, 1983), pp 1-80.

4 E W Blyden, *Christianity, Islam and the Negro Race* (London: W B Whittingham & Co, 2nd ed 1889), p 65.

5 For a judicious survey of these and other issues, see B Stanley, *The Bible and the Flag* (Leicester: Apollos, 1990).

6 On Paul's lifestyle in relation to his strategies for evangelization, cf R F Hock, *The Social Context of Paul's Ministry* (Philadelphia: Fortress, 1980).

7 *Mission and Evangelism – an ecumenical affirmation* (Geneva: WCC 1982), section 28.

8 Reported in *LandMARC* (New Year 1990), p 3.

9 Haddon Robinson, 'Listening to the Listeners', in J D Berkley (ed), *Preaching to Convince* (Waco, TX: Word, 1986), p 46.

10 On communication issues in general, see C H Kraft, *Communication Theory for Christian Witness* (Nashville: Abingdon Press, 1983), J F Engel, *Contemporary Christian Communications* (Nashville: Thomas Nelson, 1979).

Chapter 4 What is Conversion?

1 Augustine, *Confessions* viii. 12.

2 *Views from the Pews* (London: BCC and CTS, 1986), p 37.

3 John Finney, *Finding Faith Today*, pp 23–24.

4 *Finding Faith Today*, p 25. It is worth observing, however, that this research also discovered that, even in those churches with no tradition of dramatic or crisis conversion, some 20 per cent of converts actually had such an experience.

5 On the distortions this has caused, cf K Stendahl, 'Paul and the Introspective conscience of the West', in *Paul among Jews and Gentiles* (Philadelphia: Fortress Press, 1976), pp 78–96.

6 On the significance of Paul's Damascus road experience as the source of his distinctive theological understanding, see the classic work of Seyoon Kim, *The Origin of Paul's Gospel* (Grand Rapids: Eerdmans, 1982). For a briefer summary, see my *Introducing the New Testament* (Oxford: Lion, 1986), pp 361–367.

7 For one of the most striking expositions of the total and radical nature of conversion, see Jim Wallis, *The Call to Conversion* (Oxford: Lion, 1982). Wallis's work is specially instructive, as he came from a background where the single instantaneous moment of crisis was the normative view of conversion.

8 Cf T A Droege, *Faith Passages and Patterns* (Philadelphia: Fortress Press, 1983), pp 7–26.

9 'The one preaches the Gospel of bodies without souls, while the other preaches the Gospel of souls without bodies. The first is a corpse and the second a ghost.' (quoted by B Hathaway, and attributed to E Stanley Jones, in *Quadrant*, November 1993, p 5).

10 On Peter, cf Oscar Cullmann, *Peter* (London: SCM, 1962); R E Brown, K P Donfried, J Reumann, *Peter in the New Testament* (Minneapolis: Augsburg, 1973); R E Brown and J P Meier, *Antioch and Rome* (London: Geoffrey Chapman, 1983). There are of course many historical and critical questions raised by the presentation of Peter in the various New Testament books, though I believe that enough can be known about him for the purposes of charting the course of his life of discipleship. In any case, given that Peter was one of their great heroes, we may assume that the model he embodies must have represented the early Church's widely held concept of the nature of discipleship.

11 Cf Hans Ruedi Weber, *Jesus and the Children* (Geneva: WCC, 1979).

12 On this, see R A Batey, *Jesus and the Forgotten City: new light on Sepphoris and the urban world of Jesus* (Grand Rapids: Baker, 1991).

13 *Mission and Evangelism – an ecumenical affirmation*, section 7.

14 The story in John 1:35–42, though obviously from a different set of traditions, displays very similar characteristics to the story in Mark 1:16–20. In the fourth gospel, Peter shows the same motivational attachment to whatever he thinks Jesus stands for, and is following at a distance. When Jesus unexpectedly addresses him, he covers his embarrassment by asking what seems an irrelevant question ('where are you staying?') – but he still ends up going after Jesus.

15 *Mission and Evangelism – an ecumenical affirmation*, section 13.

16 W Temple, quoted in S Neill, *The Unfinished Task* (London: Lutterworth, 1957), p 45.

17 J Hagberg and R A Guelich, *The Critical Journey* (Dallas: Word, 1989), p 15.

18 Cf J Finney, *Finding Faith Today*, pp 49–50.

19 There is a vast and growing literature on this subject. Significant texts include the following: J W Fowler, *Stages of Faith* (San Francisco: Harper & Row, 1981); J W Fowler, *Becoming Adult, Being Christian* (San Francisco: Harper & Row, 1984); J W Fowler, K E Nipkow, F Schweitzer (eds), *Stages of Faith and Religious Development* (London: SCM Press, 1992); J Westerhoff III, *Will our Children Have Faith?* (San Francisco: Harper & Row, 1976); V B Gillespie, *The Experience of Faith* (Birmingham, Alabama: Religious Education Press, 1988); W E Conn, *Conversion* (New York: Alba House, 1978); J Astley and L Francis (eds), *Christian Perspectives on Faith Development* (Leominster: Gracewing / Grand Rapids: Eerdmans, 1992).

Chapter 5 Evangelism and Worship

1 *International Review of Mission* LIV (1965), p 455.

2 'To make evangelism the primary concern of the Church is to give it a misplaced and exaggerated position in our lives. The first task of the Church is to worship ... ' William Abraham, *The Logic of Evangelism* (London: Hodder & Stoughton, 1989), p 182.

3 They also raise theological questions for some people. Describing a visit to Willow Creek Community Church in Chicago, Anthony B Robinson asks, ' ... is what it offers recognizable as the church? Or has the worshipping congregation been transformed into an audience? Are the weekly services more entertainment than worship?' ('Learning from Willow Creek Church', in *Christian Century*, 23 January 1991, p 69). The same question could of course be addressed to more traditional churches as well, as we shall see later in this chapter.

4 In 1949, China had 800,000 Protestant Christians. Forty years later that had grown to 4 million, even according to the figures of an unsympathetic Chinese government. Other sources put the number closer to as many as 40 million. For a well-informed account, see Raymond Fung, *Households of God on China's Soil* (Geneva: WCC, 1982).

5 Cf C G Jung, *Modern Man in Search of a Soul* (London: Routledge and Kegan Paul, 1933); R S Valle, 'The Emergence of Transpersonal Psychology', in R S Valle and S Halling (eds), *Existential-Phenomenological Perspectives in Psychology* (New York: Plenum Press, 1989), pp 257–268.

6 Raymond Fung, *The Isaiah Vision* (Geneva: WCC, 1992), p 13.

7 Raymond Fung, *The Isaiah Vision*, p 14.

8 On this, see Robert Banks, *Going to Church in the First Century* (Parramatta NSW: Hexagon, 1985); and for a modern application of it, Robert and Julia Banks, *The Church Comes Home* (Sutherland, NSW: Albatross, 1986).

9 Ernst Käsemann, 'Ministry and Community in the New Testament', in *Essays on New Testament Themes* (London: SCM, 1963), pp 63–94 (quotation is from p 81).

10 For detailed accounts of this consult Peter Honey and Alan Mumford, *The Manual of Learning Styles* (Maidenhead: Peter Honey, 3rd ed. 1992).

11 *Finding Faith Today*, p 25.

12 William Abraham, *The Logic of Evangelism*, p 171.

13 There was no shortage of people even in the early centuries who found all this highly threatening, of course. Docetists and Gnostics soon began to deny that Jesus could possibly have been fully divine from his birth, and instead saw him as receiving a divine spirit at baptism, or on some other occasion. In practice, if not in theory, quite a few Christians today are crypto-gnostics on such matters, which probably explains the almost total absense of any satisfactory theology of childhood in all our traditions.

14 Ian Wray, 'Buddhism and Psychotherapy', in G Claxton, *Beyond Therapy* (London: Wisdom Publications, 1986), pp 160–161.

15 Raymond Fung, *The Isaiah Vision*, pp 14–15.

16 John Naisbitt and Patricia Aburdene, *Megatrends 2000* (London: Pan, 1991), pp 53–76.

17 *Epistle to Diognetus* 5.

18 Michael Marshall, *Renewal in Worship* (London: Marshall, Morgan & Scott, 1982), p 65.

Chapter 6 Evangelizing Strategies for the Local Church

1 By 1989, though, there was a more circumspect understanding of what this might mean, and even in the opening address of the Lausanne II Congress, chairperson Leighton Ford admitted that 'It is even possible that Jesus Christ may do this greatest work through some people who aren't at this Congress and might never be invited.' See J D Douglas (ed), *Proclaim Christ Until He Comes* (Minneapolis: World Wide Publications, 1990). Quotation from p 54. The note of realism was even more pronounced at the parallel CFWM conference held in San Antonio the same year under the auspices of the World Council of Churches.

2 On the way in which these incidents might be fitted into the overall context of Paul's life, see my *Introducing the New Testament*, pp 277–280; D A Carson, D J Moo and L Morris, *An Introduction to the New Testament* (Leicester: Apollos, 1992), pp 223–231, 289–296.

3 On the wider issues relating to how we may date Paul's life, see G Lüdemann, *Paul Apostle to the Gentiles: studies in Chronology* (London: SCM Press, 1984); R Jewett, *Dating Paul's Life* (London: SCM Press, 1979).

4 For the evangelistic relevance of church planning, see Jeffrey Harris, 'Structural Considerations', in M Hill (ed), *Entering the Kingdom* (London: MARC Europe, 1986), pp 69–83.

5 The emperor Claudius formally excluded the Jews from Rome in AD 49, and it was several years later before his successor Nero allowed them back again (Suetonius, *Life of Claudius* 25.4). In an edict to the inhabitants of Alexandria in Egypt, the same Claudius described the Jews as 'a general plague throughout the world'. Many Greek writers of the time depicted the Jews in a bad light. For a particularly extensive catalogue of anti-semitic misinformation, see the Latin author Tacitus *History* V.1–13.

6 Gilbert Murray once described it as a 'failure of nerve': 'It is hard to describe. It is a rise of asceticism, of mysticism, in a sense, of pessimism; a loss of self-confidence, of hope in this life and of faith in normal human effort; a despair of patient enquiry, a cry for infallible revelation; an indifference to the welfare of the state, a conversion of the soul to God.' (*Five Stages of Greek Religion*, Oxford: OUP, 1925, p 155). This diagnosis of the spiritual condition of the Hellenistic age has more than a few similarities with the spiritual climate of western culture today – something which ought to give us confidence (if we needed it) to root our solutions firmly in the New Testament.

7 On Paul's creative use of the letter form, see W G Doty, *Letters in Primitive Christianity* (Philadelphia: Fortress Press, 1973).

8 Quoted in James D Berkley (ed), *Preaching to Convince*, p 41.

9 I have no problem about applying the term 'power evangelism' to such an encounter, though I would not share the opinion of those who imply that every evangelistic opportunity has this character (cf J Wimber and K Springer, *Power Evangelism*, London: Hodder & Stoughton, 1985). Part of the reason for Paul's extraordinary success was his ability to be flexible, utilizing different approaches on different occasions.

10 For more on this, and a comparison of the evangelizing styles of Paul and Jesus, see my 'Patterns of Evangelization in Paul and Jesus: a way forward in the Jesus-Paul debate?' in J B Green and M M B Turner, *Jesus of Nazareth, Lord and Christ* (Grand Rapids: Eerdmans, 1994), pp 281–296.

11 R Fung, 'Mission in Christ's Way', in *International Review of Mission* LXXIX (1990), p 8.

12 M Green, *Evangelism Now and Then* (Leicester: IVP, 1979), pp 33–52; M Green, *Evangelism through the Local Church* (London: Hodder & Stoughton, 1990), pp 82–103.

13 The expression of John P Meier, *Antioch and Rome*, p 12. For a succinct account of Christianity in Antioch, see also W Meeks and R Wilken, *Jews and Christians in Antioch* (Missoula: Scholars Press 1978).

14 *Essays on New Testament Themes*, pp 80–81. For further evidence, Käsemann draws attention not only to 1 Corinthians 12, but also 1 Peter 2:5–10. This is not an eccentric view: mainstream New Testament scholarship would agree with it. James Dunn's comments are typical: 'There is no such thing as passive membership ... to belong to the body is to have a function within the body, a contribution which the member must make ... the idea of mono-ministry, of all the most important gifts concentrated on one man (even an apostle) is foolish nonsense to Paul ... Paul has no concept of a hierarchy of offices.' See his *Jesus and the Spirit* (London: SCM Press, 1975), quotations from pp 264, 268.

15 On such organizations in general, see Charles Handy, *Understanding Voluntary Organizations* (London: Penguin, 1990).

16 Bryant Myers, 'Christian leadership in the nineties', in *MARC Newsletter* 91/1 (March 1991), p 3.

17 R Ackoff, *Creating the Corporate Future*, p 30.

18 R Ackoff, *Creating the Corporate Future*, p 33.

19 For some of this, see Charles Handy, *The Age of Unreason*, pp 137–402.

20 R Fung, 'Mission in Christ's Way', pp 8–13, 16–17; *The Isaiah Vision*, especially pp 43–47.

21 For more on this concept from a management point of view, cf Charles

Handy, *Understanding Organizations* (London: Penguin, 4th ed. 1993) – though he observes that even the 'stakeholder' model will soon be forced towards a more genuine sense of community ownership and accountability: 'In order to give proper expression to the ideas of stakeholders and community the power of ownership will not ... reside in the centre but in the parts ... making the centre truly the servant of the whole, not the master of it.' (p 366). For Christians to grasp that would require a major change in our present attitudes to non-church culture, as well as (encouragingly) a return to some fundamental values espoused by Jesus.

22 Jim Dethmer (a leader in Willow Creek Community Church, Chicago), quoted by Russell Chandler, *Racing Toward 2001*, p 210.

23 *Mission and Evangelism – an ecumenical affirmation*, Preface.

24 J Needleman, *Lost Christianity*, quotations from p 35 and p 4.

25 Roland Allen, *Missionary Methods: St Paul's or Ours?* (Grand Rapids: Eerdmans, 1962; originally published in 1912). See also David Paton and Charles H Long (eds), *The Compulsion of the Spirit: a Roland Allen Reader* (Grand Rapids: Eerdmans, 1983).

26 Foreword to the 1962 edition of *Missionary Methods: St Paul's or Ours?* pp i-iii. John Stott also comments that Allen's 'principles have been remarkably vindicated in recent years', see his *Message of Acts* (Leicester: IVP, 1990), p 235.

27 On Paul's relations with Jerusalem, see B Holmberg, *Paul and Power* (Lund: CWK Gleerup, 1978).

28 Cf J D G Dunn, *Unity and Diversity in the New Testament* (London: SCM Press, 1977). According to some, the diversity was more than merely cultural: cf W Bauer, *Orthodoxy and Heresy in Earliest Christianity* (London: SCM Press, 1972).

29 A Maslow, *Toward a Psychology of Being* (New York: Van Nostrand Reinhold, 2nd ed. 1968).

Chapter 7 Putting it into Practice

1 D Bonhoeffer, *Life Together* (London: SCM Press, 1954), p 75.

2 Not quite always. It will do us no harm to reflect on the fact that out of all the people Jesus met, the only ones he consistently put down were the Pharisees – and they were religious types, like us.

3 See R Fung for other examples from around the world ('Mission in Christ's Way', pp 20–23; *The Isaiah Vision*, pp 17–18, 29–31, 36–37, 40).

4 Luther, quoted in J D Berkley, *Preaching to Convince*, p 113.

5 On this understanding of Luke 15 and the two dynamics of going and waiting, see R Fung, 'Mission in Christ's Way', pp 6–9.

6 *Mission and Evangelism – an ecumenical affirmation*, sections 41, 43.

Appendix 1 Conversion and Faith Development

1 Janet Hagberg and Robert Guelich, *The Critical Journey*, p 7.

2 Cf E L Hayes, 'The Biblical Foundations of Christian Education', in W Graendorf, *Introduction to Biblical Christian Education* (Chicago: Moody, 1981). William Barclay, *Educational Ideals of the Ancient World* (Grand Rapids: Baker, 1974).

3 J Wilhoit, *Christian Education and the Search for Meaning* (Grand Rapids: Baker, 1986), p 22. See also V B Gillespie, *Religious Conversion and Personal Identity* (Birmingham, Alabama: Religious Education Press, 1979), a study which integrates 'conversion' as part of the life cycle itself.

4 Erikson's concept of the 'eight ages of man' was a useful starting point, though it was Kohlberg's notion of six stages of moral development that provided the structure for Fowler's own theory of 'stages of faith'. Cf Fowler, *Stages of Faith*, pp 98–105. In *The Psychology of Moral Development* (San Francisco: Harper & Row, 1981), L Kohlberg himself tentatively proposes the addition of a seventh stage, which in his terms would be a 'religious' stage.

5 For other selected contributions to the discussion, see note 19 in chapter 4.

6 W Cantwell Smith, *Faith and Belief* (Princeton: Princeton University Press, 1979).

7 In biblical Hebrew, faith is never a noun, always a verb: cf James Barr, *The Semantics of Biblical Language* (Oxford: OUP, 1961), pp 161–205.

8 C E Nelson questions Fowler's definition of faith, claiming 'It is noteworthy that the Hebrew word for faith is never used for faith in false gods' (*How Faith Matures*, p 238). This is a significant question for exegesis, though it is not strictly relevant to understanding faith in the context of evangelization, especially in the light of the biblical models provided by Jesus and Paul.

9 Cf Carol Gilligan, in J W Fowler, *Becoming Adult, Being Christian*, p 38.

10 Cf C E Nelson, 'Does Faith Develop? An evaluation of Fowler's position', in *The Living Light* 19 (1982), pp 162–173.

11 N Q Hamilton, *Maturing in the Christian Life: A Pastor's Guide* (Philadelphia: Geneva Press, 1984).

12 J Hagberg and R Guelich, *The Critical Journey*, p xv.

13 *The Critical Journey*, p 4.

14 R Moseley, in a 1978 Harvard dissertation referred to by Fowler, *Stages of Faith*, pp 285–286. See also Fowler, *Becoming Adult, Being Christian*, pp 138–141.

15 Fowler, 'Faith and the structuring of meaning', in Fowler, Vergote, Brusselmans (eds), *Toward Moral and Religious Maturity* (Morristown, NJ: Silver Burdett Co., 1980), p 67.

16 See James E Loder, *The Transforming Moment: Understanding Convictional Experiences* (San Francisco: Harper & Row, 1989), pp 97–115. See also J E Loder and J W Fowler, 'Conversations on Fowler's Stages of Faith and Loder's The Transforming Moment, in *Religious Education* 77/2 (1982), pp 133–148.